Fodor's P O C K E T 2nd edition

mexico
CITY

G000019834

Excerpted from *Fodor's Mexico*
fodor's travel publications
new york · toronto · london · sydney · auckland
www.fodors.com

contents

On the Road with Fodor's *iv*

Don't Forget to Write *v*

maps

ON THE ROAD WITH FODOR'S

WE'VE PULLED OUT ALL STOPS in preparing *Fodor's Pocket Mexico City*. To guide you in putting together your Mexico City experience, we've created multiday itineraries and regional tours. And to direct you to the places that are truly worth your time and money, we've rallied the team of endearingly picky know-it-alls we're pleased to call our writers. Having seen all corners of Mexico City, they're real experts. If you knew them, you'd poll them for tips yourself.

So drawn to the surrealism of Mexico that she turned a one-week vacation into a 20-year sojourn, **Patricia Alisau** has traveled just about every inch of the country on assignment for Mexican and U.S. journals. She has written for Mexico's *Vogue* magazine and, as a foreign correspondent, for the *New York Times*, the *Chicago Tribune*, and the Associated Press. She updated the Practical Information, Eating Out, and Where to Stay sections of this edition.

The information in these pages is largely the work of **Paige Bierma**, who covers political and social issues for major U.S. newspapers and magazines. After working as a reporter for several years in her native Iowa and in California, she headed south of the border to bring Mexican news to the breakfast tables of the north-of-the-border public. It took her six years to leave.

Don't Forget to Write

Keeping a travel guide fresh and up-to-date is a big job. So we love your feedback—positive and negative—and follow up on all suggestions. Contact the *Pocket Mexico City* editor at editorsfodors.com or c/o Fodor's, 280 Park Avenue, New York, New York 10017. And have a wonderful trip!

Karen Cure

[signature]

Editorial Director

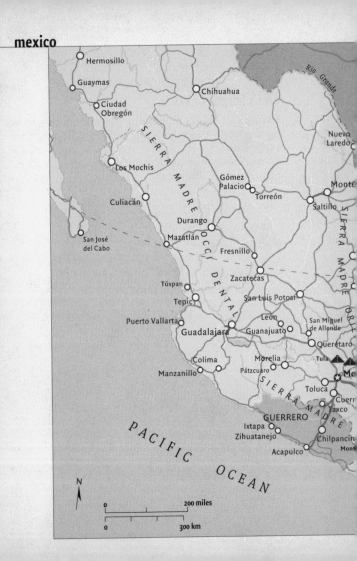

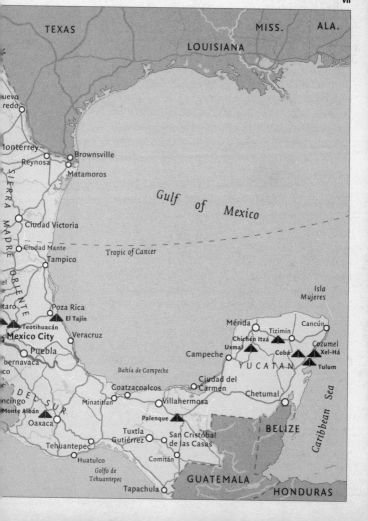

mexico
CITY

In This Chapter

By Frank Shiell
Updated by Paige Bierma

introducing
mexico city

MEXICO CITY IS A CITY OF SUPERLATIVES: It is both the oldest (670 years) and the highest (7,349 ft) city on the North American continent. And with nearly 24 million inhabitants, it is the most populous city in the world. It is Mexico's cultural, political, and financial core—on the verge of the 21st century but clinging to its deeply entrenched Aztec heritage.

As the gargantuan pyramids of Teotihuacán attest—the name is Aztec, meaning "the place where one becomes a god"—the area around Mexico City was occupied from early times by a great civilization, probably Nahuatl in origin. The founding of the Aztec capital nearby did not occur until more than 600 years after Teotihuacán was abandoned, around 750. As the story goes, the nomadic Aztecs were searching for a promised land in which to settle. Their prophesies said they would recognize the spot when they encountered an eagle, perched on a prickly-pear cactus, holding a snake in its beak. In 1325, the disputed date given for the founding of the city of Tenochtitlán, the Aztecs discovered this eagle in the valley of Mexico. They built Tenochtitlán on what was then an island in shallow Lake Texcoco and connected it to lakeshore satellite towns by a network of *calzadas* (canals and causeways, now freeways). Even then it was the largest city in the Western hemisphere and, according to historians, one of the three largest cities on earth. When he first laid eyes on Tenochtitlán in the 16th century,

Spanish conquistador Hernán Cortés was dazzled by the glistening metropolis, which reminded him of Venice.

A combination of factors made the conquest possible. The superstitious Aztec emperor Moctezuma II believed the white, bearded Cortés on horseback to be the mighty plumed serpent-god Quetzalcóatl, who, according to a tragically ironic prophesy, was supposed to arrive from the east in the year 1519 to rule the land. Moctezuma therefore welcomed the foreigner with gifts of gold and palatial accommodations.

But in return, Cortés initiated the bloody massacre of Tenochtitlán, which lasted almost two years. Joining forces with him was a massive army of Indian "allies," gathered from other settlements like Cholula and Tlaxcala, who were fed up with the Aztec empire's domination and with paying tribute, especially sending warriors and maidens to be sacrificed. With the strength of their numbers and the European tactical advantages of brigantines built to cross the lake, imported horses, firearms, armor, and, inadvertently, smallpox and the common cold, Cortés succeeded in devastating Tenochtitlán. Only two centuries after it was founded, the young Aztec capital lay in ruins, about half of its population dead from battle, starvation, and contagious European diseases against which they had no immunity.

Cortés began building the capital of what he patriotically dubbed New Spain, the Spanish empire's colony that would spread north to cover what is now the United States southwest, and south to Panama. Mexico comes from the word Mexica (pronounced meh-shee-ka), which is the Aztec name for themselves. Aztec is the Spaniards' name for the Mexica. At the site of the demolished Aztec ceremonial center—now the 10-acre Zócalo—Cortés started building a church (the precursor of the gigantic Metropolitan Cathedral), mansions, and government buildings. He utilized the slave labor—and artistry—of the vanquished native Mexicans. On top of the ruins of their city, and using rubble from it, they were forced to build what became the most European-style city in North America. But instead of having the random layout of contemporary medieval European cities, it followed the sophisticated grid pattern of the Aztecs. The Spaniards also drained and filled in Lake Texcoco, preferring wheels and horses (which they introduced to Mexico) over canals and canoes for transport. The land-filled lake bed turned out to be a soggy support for the immense buildings that have been slowly sinking into it ever since they were built. For much of the construction material the Spaniards quarried the local porous, volcanic, dried-blood-colored stone called *tezontle*, which forms the thick walls of many historic buildings downtown.

During the colonial period the city grew, and the Franciscans and Dominicans converted the Aztecs to Christianity. In 1571 the Spaniards established the Inquisition in New Spain and burned heretics at its palace headquarters, which still stands in Plaza de Santo Domingo.

It took more than 200 years for Mexicans to successfully rise up against Spain. The historic downtown street 16 de Septiembre commemorates the "declaration" of the War of Independence. On that date in 1810, Father Miguel Hidalgo rang a church bell and cried out his history-making *grito* (shout): "Viva Ferdinand VII [king of Spain at the time]! Death to bad government!" Some historians conclude that Hidalgo's call to arms in the name of the Spanish monarch was just a facade to start an independence movement, which Hidalgo successfully accomplished. That "liberty bell," which now hangs above the main entrance to the National Palace, is rung on every eve of September 16 by the president of the republic, who then shouts a revised version of the patriot's cry: "Viva Mexico! Viva Mexico! Viva Mexico!"

Now, flying in or out of Mexico City, you'll get an aerial view of the remaining part of Lake Texcoco on the eastern outskirts of the city. At night the expanse of city lights abruptly ends at a black void that appears to be an ocean. In daylight you can also see the sprawling flatness of the 1,482-square-km (572-square-mi) *Meseta de Anáhuac* (Valley of Mexico), completely surrounded by mountains. On its south side, two supposedly extinct and usually snowcapped volcanoes, Popocatépetl and Iztaccíhuatl, are both well over 17,000 ft high. After a nine-month trek from Veracruz, Cortés had his first astonishing glimpse of Tenochtitlán from the 4-km-high (2½-mi-high) pass between these mountains.

Unfortunately, the single most widely known fact about Mexico City is that its air is polluted. So you might picture the city, its streets packed with vehicles, wrapped daily in a cloak of black smog. In reality, in spite of the capital's serious pollution problem, it also has some of the clearest, bluest skies anywhere. At 7,349 ft, it often has mild daytime weather perfect for sightseeing and cool evenings comfortable for sleeping. Mornings can be glorious—chilly and bright with the promise of the warming sun.

If Mexico City's smog brings Los Angeles to mind, so might the fault line that runs through the valley. In 1957 a major earthquake took a tragic toll, and scars are still visible from the devastating 1985 earthquake—8.1 on the Richter scale. The government reported 10,000 deaths, but the word around town put the toll at 50,000.

Growing nonstop, Mexico City covers about a 1,000-square-km (386-square-mi) area of the valley. The city is surrounded on three sides by the state of Mexico and bordered on the south by the state of Morelos. Glossy magazine ads usually tout Mexico's paradisiacal beach resorts and ancient ruins, but cosmopolitan, historic Mexico City is a vital destination in itself—more fascinating than many major capitals on faraway continents.

–Frank "Pancho" Shiell

PLEASURES AND PASTIMES

Dining

Mexico City has been a culinary capital ever since the time of Moctezuma. Chronicles tell of the extravagant daily banquets prepared for the slender Aztec emperor by his palace chefs. More than 300 different dishes were served for every meal—vast assortments of meat and fowl seasoned in dozens of ways; limitless fruit, vegetables, and herbs; freshwater fish; and fresh seafood that was rushed to Tenochtitlán from both seacoasts by sprinting relay runners.

Until the 15th century, Europeans had never seen indigenous Mexican edibles such as corn, chilies of all varieties, tomatoes, potatoes, pumpkin, squash, avocado, turkey, cacao (chocolate), and vanilla. In turn, the colonization brought European gastronomic influence and ingredients—wheat, onions, garlic, olives, citrus fruit, cattle, sheep, goats, chickens, domesticated pigs (and lard for frying)—and ended up broadening the already complex pre-Hispanic cuisine into one of the most multifaceted and exquisite in the world: traditional Mexican.

Today's cosmopolitan Mexico City is a gastronomic melting pot with some 15,000 restaurants. You'll find everything from simple family-style eateries to five-star world-class restaurants. And international restaurants serve foods from around the world—although Spanish and French haute-cuisine are dominant.

In the past decade or so a renaissance of Mexican cooking has brought about a new wave known as *cocina mexicana moderna* (modern Mexican cuisine), which many Mexico City restaurants serve. Emphasis is on presentation, the delicate tastes of traditional regional dishes gleaned from colonial cookbooks, and ancient indigenous cooking techniques such as steaming and baking, which used a lot less fat, as there were no pigs for lard. Also, items such as crunchy fried grasshoppers and cooked *maguey* (cactus) worms now grace the menus of the best restaurants in town.

Lodging

As might be expected of a megalopolis, Mexico City has more than 25,000 hotel rooms—enough to accommodate every taste and budget. You can lodge in the quaint or the colonial, the smoked-glass-and-steel high-rise, or the elegant replica of an Italianate palace.

Museums

Mexico City is the cultural as well as political capital of the country, as evidenced by its 80-plus museums—some of the finest in Latin America. In buildings of architectural merit, you can see the sweeping murals of such native sons as Diego Rivera, José Clemente Orozco, and Juan O'Gorman; the gripping surrealism of Frida Kahlo; stunning pre-Hispanic ceremonial pieces; and outstanding collections of religious art.

Nightlife and the Arts

Mexico City is the cultural capital of Latin America and, with the exception of Río de Janiero, has the liveliest nightlife of the region. There's something for every taste, from opera and symphonies to a renowned folklore ballet and a lively square where mariachi play. You'll also find discos and offbeat places where salsa and *danzón* (Cuban dance music) are headliners.

Shopping

Native crafts and specialties from all over Mexico are available in the capital, as are designer clothes. You'll also find modern art by some of the best contemporary painters, many of whom are making a name for themselves in the United States. And of course Mexican goods are a far better deal here than they are in overseas outlets.

Sports and the Outdoors

Latin sports such as the *fiesta brava* (bullfighting)—brought to Mexico by the conquistadores—have enjoyed popularity for more than four centuries in the capital, which attracts the country's best athletes. And although the roots of soccer ("fútbol") are probably English, a weekend afternoon game at Mexico City's giant Estadio Azteca leaves no question that this is the sport Mexicans are craziest about. Adventure-travel agencies have also opened in Mexico City to offer great weekend getaways such as white-water rafting in nearby Veracruz. Tennis, golf, running—even rowing a boat in a park—are other outdoor pursuits to engage in while in town.

QUICK TOURS

If you're here for just a short period you need to plan carefully so you don't miss the must-see sights. The following itineraries will help you structure your visit efficiently. See Here and There for more information about individual sights.

Tour One: The Zócalo

An excellent point of departure for any tour of the city's center is the **Zócalo,** the heart and soul of old downtown. From here you can literally see the layers of history in the buildings around you. On the north side of this huge square you'll see the tilting **Catedral Metropolitana** and adjacent to it the comparatively small 18th-century Sagrario Chapel, even more angled than the cathedral. The **Templo Mayor,** ruins from the Aztec capital, is northeast of the cathedral, across the pedestrian plaza. If you're interested in modern art, walk south about half a block from the Templo Mayor to the end of Calle Seminario, then go two blocks east on Calle Moneda to Academia to find the **Museo José Luis Cuevas.** Take Moneda back (west) to the Zócalo. The first building you'll see on your left is the massive **Palacio Nacional,** covering two city blocks. Walk south past the palacio to the corner and turn right, crossing the street to get to the section of the Zócalo occupied by the 1722 **Ayuntamiento.** Recross the street and walk northwest through the open square to Calle Cinco de Mayo and the National Pawn Shop in the **Monte de Piedad.** Three-and-a-half blocks north is the historic **Plaza de Santo Domingo.** Walk one block east along Calle República de Cuba and one block south on Calle República de Argentina to get to Calle Justo Sierra and the **Conjunto de San Idelfonso,** now an art gallery. Turn west and follow Calle Justo Sierra three blocks—it will change into Calle Donceles—to Calle República de Chile, then turn left (south) a block to Calle Tacuba. Turn right and walk one block to have a scrumptious lunch at the Café de Tacuba (☞ Eating Out) on the right side of the street.

The streets in the walking tour are fairly close to one another and can be covered in half a day. The National Palace, Templo Mayor and its museum, and the Conjunto de San Idelfonso are each worth an hour of your time.

Tour Two: Alameda Central

Start off on Calle Madero, one of the city's most architecturally varied streets. On the south side of Madero, between Bolivar and Gante, is the 1780 Baroque **Palacio de Iturbide.** Go west along on the south side of Madero; less than a block past the palacio you'll come to the **Iglesia de San Francisco,** with its beautifully painted walls. The stunning tilework of the **Casa de los Azulejos** will draw your eye across Calle Madero.

From Calle Madero, walk less than a half block west to Eje Central Lázaro Cárdenas, a wide four-lane avenue. At the corner and on your left, you can't miss the 1950s-style skyscraper, the **Torre Latinoamericana,** which has one of the best aerial views of the city as well as a sky-high aquarium. Cross the avenue and turn right (north) to explore the beautiful **Palacio de Bellas Artes** opera house, the long side of which skirts Lázaro

Cárdenas (its entrance is on Juárez). The 1908 post-office building of **Dirección General de Correos** is up Lázaro Cárdenas another 150 ft across from Bellas Artes.

Pass the post office to Calle Tacuba and walk east two blocks to visit the **Museo Nacional de Arte** in the colonial Plaza Manuel Tolsa. Back on Calle Tacuba, head west and cross Lázaro Cárdenas one last time, where Calle Tacuba turns into Avenida Hidalgo. A few blocks walk will bring you to the antique-filled **Museo Franz Mayer.** Across Avenida Hidalgo is the north end of the leafy park **Alameda Central.** At its south end, on Avenida Juárez, **Fonart** is a government-owned handicrafts store (☞ Shopping). To get to the **Museo Mural Diego Rivera,** take Juárez west to Calle Balderas, about 3½ blocks from Fonart. Turn right and walk a short block to Calle Colón.

The streets in this tour are also fairly close to one another. Leave about a half-hour each for the Palacio de Bellas Artes (unless there's an exhibition that particularly interests you), the Museo Mural Diego Rivera, and Fonart, and an hour each for the Museo Nacional de Arte and the Museo Franz Mayer.

Tour Three: Zona Rosa, Bosque de Chapultepec, and Colonia Condesa

Start your exploration of the Zona Rosa section at the junction of Reforma, Avenida Juárez, and Bucareli, just west of the Alameda Central. Along the stretch of Reforma west of this intersection are a number of statues erected at the request of former Mexican president Porfirio Díaz to honor illustrious men, including Simón Bolívar, Columbus, Pasteur, and the Aztec emperor Cuauhtémoc. The best known, the **Monumento a la Independencia,** also known as The Angel, marks the western edge of the Zona Rosa. To get the best of the area's sights, walk along Hamburgo, Londres, and Copenhague streets—like others in the Zona, named for Continental cities. There is a crafts market, Mercado Zona Rosa, on Londres.

Four blocks southwest of the Zona Rosa, at Avenida Chapultepec, you'll come to the main entrance of **Bosque de Chapultepec,** or Chapultepec Park. Uphill from the entrance is the **Castillo de Chapultepec** and its National History Museum. Heading downhill again after leaving the Castillo, you'll go past the much smaller, also historical, **Museo del Caracol.** North of the Castillo on the near side of Paseo de la Reforma is the **Museo de Arte Moderno.** Almost directly across Paseo de la Reforma on its north side and west of Calle Gandhi, you'll see the **Museo Rufino Tamayo,** in which you'll find Tamayo's works as well as those of other modern artists. West of the Museo Tamayo on the same side of Reforma is the **Museo Nacional de Antropología,** with its world-renowned collections of Mesoamerican art and artifacts. Cross Reforma again and you'll come to the entrance to the **Zoológico.**

Southeast of Bosque de Chapultepec, **Colonia Condesa** is a tree-lined neighborhood where meandering streets make for pleasant strolling, especially in spring when jacaranda blossoms color the colonia. From the Bosque de Chapultepec, take a *pesero* (minibus) from beside the Chapultepec metro or a five-minute taxi ride to the trendy restaurant zone of Calle Michoacán. If you choose to walk, it'll take 15–20 minutes: walk up Calle Veracruz going away from the park, turn right on Avenida Mazatlán, then left onto Calle Michoacán.

If you only visit one of these museums, make it the National Museum of Anthropology. You'll need two hours for even a quick go-through. (To really appreciate the fine exhibits, anywhere from a half-day to two full days is more appropriate.) You can easily spend an hour at each of the other Bosque de Chapultepec museums. On Sunday and Mexican holidays, when museum entry is free, the park and museums are packed with families. Adding Colonia Condesa to the end of a day of museum visits will make for a delightful evening.

Tour Four: San Angel and Coyoacán

To explore the southern part of the city take a taxi or pesero down Avenida Insurgentes and get off at Avenida La Paz. On the east side of Insurgentes is the **Monumento al General Alvaro Obregón.** Cross Insurgentes on Avenida La Paz, and take the southern fork off Avenida La Paz (Calle Madero) until you come to San Angel's center, **Plaza San Jacinto.** Stroll to the **Casa del Risco** on the north side of the plaza and, if it's a Saturday, head for the **Bazar Sábado** (☞ Markets in Shopping) on the north end. Retrace your steps on Avenida La Paz, to Avenida Revolución and Plaza del Carmen, which lies at the corner of Calle Monasterio. Inside is the colonial **Ex-Convento del Carmen,** interesting as an example of sacred architecture and for its religious artifacts. Now take Avenida Revolución one long block north to see the modern Mexican and European works at the **Museo Alvar y Carmen T. de Carrillo Gil.**

The next part of the tour goes to Coyoacán, which extends east of Avenida Insurgentes about 1 km (½ mi) from San Angel. Consider taking a taxi to the Plaza de Santa Catarina on Avenida Francisco Sosa, about halfway into the center of Coyoacán, because the tour involves a lot of walking.

If you decide to hoof it, make your way east to the corner of Avenidas Universidad and Francisco Sosa. Head east on Francisco Sosa until you come to the pretty 16th-century Iglesia de Santa Catarina, which dominates the tiny **Plaza de Santa Catarina.** The plaza also contains a bust of Mexican historian Francisco Sosa, who lived here and wrote passionately about Coyoacán. Across the street is the **Casa de Jesús Reyes Heroles** (Avenida Francisco Sosa 202); the former home of the ex-minister of education is a fine example of 20th-century architecture on the colonial model. It's now used as a cultural center. Continue east on Francisco Sosa and you'll pass Casa de Diego de Ordaz at the corner of Tres Cruces. This mudéjar (Spanish-Arabic) structure, adorned with inlaid tiles, was the home of a former captain in Cortés's army.

Now you're standing at the entrance of the **Jardín Centenario**. The Templo de San Juan Bautista and the picturesque **Casa de Cortés** sit in the small Plaza Hidalgo adjacent to and north of the garden. Walk two blocks southeast of Plaza Hidalgo on Calle Higuera to the corner of Calle Vallarta, where you'll find the **Casa de la Malinche.** The house, darkened with age, faces an attractive park called Plaza de la Conchita.

Return to Plaza Hidalgo and walk five blocks north on Calle Allende to the corner of Calle Londres and the **Museo de Frida Kahlo.** It's linked historically—or should we say romantically— with the fortresslike **Museo de Leon Trotsky,** east of it on Londres, then two long blocks north on Morelos.

You're likely to want to linger in these elegant and beautiful sections of town, especially in Coyoacán. The Frida Kahlo and Leon Trotsky museums give intense, intimate looks at the lives of two famous people who were friends and lovers, and who breathed their personalities into the places where they lived. Allow at least an hour at each. The other museums are much smaller and merit less time. Weekends are liveliest at the Plaza Hidalgo and its neighboring Jardín Centenario, where street life explodes into a fiesta.

Your checklist for a perfect journey

WAY AHEAD
- Devise a trip budget.
- Write down the five things you want most from this trip. Keep this list handy before and during your trip.
- Make plane or train reservations. Book lodging and rental cars.
- Arrange for pet care.
- Check your passport. Apply for a new one if necessary.
- Photocopy important documents and store in a safe place.

A MONTH BEFORE
- Make restaurant reservations and buy theater and concert tickets. Visit fodors.com for links to local events.
- Familiarize yourself with the local language or lingo.

TWO WEEKS BEFORE
- Replenish your supply of medications.
- Create your itinerary.
- Enjoy a book or movie set in your destination to get you in the mood.

- Develop a packing list. Shop for missing essentials. Repair and launder or dry-clean your clothes.

A WEEK BEFORE
- Stop newspaper deliveries. Pay bills.
- Acquire traveler's checks.
- Stock up on film.
- Label your luggage.
- Finalize your packing list— take less than you think you need.
- Create a toiletries kit filled with travel-size essentials.
- Get lots of sleep. Don't get sick before your trip.

A DAY BEFORE
- Drink plenty of water.
- Check your travel documents.
- Get packing!

DURING YOUR TRIP
- Keep a journal/scrapbook.
- Spend time with locals.
- Take time to explore. Don't plan too much.

In This Chapter

Updated by Paige Bierma

here and there

MOST OF MEXICO CITY IS ALIGNED on two major intersecting thoroughfares: Paseo de la Reforma and Avenida Insurgentes—at 34 km (21 mi), the longest avenue in the city. Administratively, Mexico City is divided into 16 *delegaciones* (districts) and about 400 *colonias* (neighborhoods), each with street names fitting a given theme, such as a river, philosopher, doctor, or revolutionary hero. The same street can change names as it goes through different colonias. Hence, most street addresses include their colonia (abbreviated as Col.). And, unless you're going to an obvious place, it is important to tell your taxi driver the name of the colonia.

The principal sights of Mexico City fall into three areas. Allow a full day to cover each thoroughly, although you could race through them in four or five hours apiece. You can cover the first two areas—the Zócalo and Alameda Central, and Zona Rosa and Bosque de Chapultepec (Chapultepec Park)—on foot. Getting around Coyoacán and San Angel in southern Mexico City will require a taxi ride or two.

Numbers in the text correspond to numbers in the margin and on the Zócalo and Alameda Central; Zona Rosa, Bosque de Chapultepec, and Colonia Condesa; and San Angel and Coyoacán maps.

THE ZÓCALO AND ALAMEDA CENTRAL

This area is all about history: the Zócalo, its surrounding Centro Histórico, and Alameda Park were the heart of both the Aztec and Spanish cities. Many of the streets in downtown Mexico City

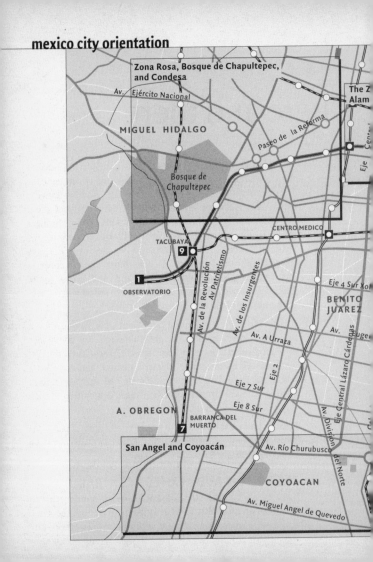

Zona Rosa, Bosque de Chapultepec, and Condesa

Av. Ejército Nacional

MIGUEL HIDALGO

Paseo de la Reforma

Bosque de Chapultepec

The Z
Alam

Eje Cent

CENTRO MEDICO

TACUBAYA

9

1

OBSERVATORIO

Av. de la Revolución

Av. Patriotismo

Av. de los Insurgentes

Eje 4 Sur Xo

BENITO
JUAREZ

Av.

uge

Av. A Urraza

Eje 2

Eje Central Lázaro Cárdenas

Eje 7 Sur

Eje 8 Sur

A. OBREGON

BARRANCA DEL
MUERTO

7

Av. División del Norte

San Angel and Coyoacán

Av. Río Churubusco

COYOACAN

Av. Miguel Angel de Quevedo

The Zócalo and
Alameda Central

Eje Central
Lázaro Cárdenas

Eje 1 Ote.

Eje 3 Ote.

Circuito

Oceanía

Interior

Aeropuerto
Internacional
Benito Juárez

V. CARRANZA

CUAUHTEMOC

Fray Servando
Teresa de Mier

Ignacio Zaragoza

PANTITLAN

1 5 9

115

Metro Ligero

SANTA ANITA

Eje 3 Sur

TOWARD PUEBLA

je 4 Sur Xola

Eje 4 Sur

IZTACALCO

ENITO
JAREZ

av.

Eugenia

Av. Plutarco Elías Calles

Eje 1 Ote.

Calz. de la Viga

Eje 5 Sur

Circuito Interior

Av. Río Churubusco

Rojo Gómez

Eje central Lázaro Cárdenas

Calz. de Tlalpan

Eje 6 Sur

Av. Cinco

Eje 2 Ote.

Av. Lic Javier

el Norte

Country
Club

Eje 3 Ote.

Parque Nacional
Cerro de la Estrella

TASQUEÑA

do

2

Calz. Tasqueña

mexico city subways

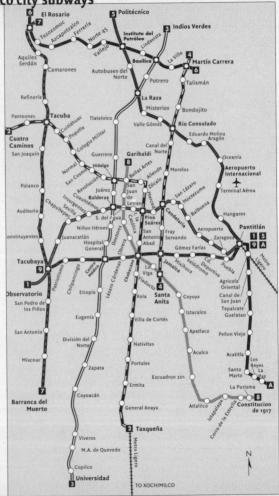

have been converted into pedestrian-only thoroughfares.

The Zócalo area is quietest on Sunday, when bureaucrats have their day of rest. But Alameda Park will be jumping with children and their parents enjoying a Sunday outing. The park will be particularly festive during Christmas, when dozens of "Santas" will appear with plastic reindeer to take wish lists from long lines of children. Although Mexicans do celebrate on Dec. 25, the traditional Mexican Christmas kicks in January 5, the eve of the Day of the Three Kings, and the Three Wise Men of biblical lore replace the Santas in the Alameda. Gorgeous Christmas paintings-in-lights deck the Zócalo from end to end and stream up Calle Madero past Alameda Park to Paseo de la Reforma beyond the museums in Bosque de Chapultepec.

During the daytime, the downtown area is filled with people and vibrant with activity. As in any big city, watch out for pickpockets, especially on crowded buses and subways, and avoid dark, deserted streets at night.

Sights to See

THE ZÓCALO

❻ AYUNTAMIENTO (City Hall). The two buildings of Mexico's city hall stand on the south side of the Zócalo; colonial tiles of the arms of Cortés and other conquistadores decorate the one on the west. Originally built in 1532, it was destroyed by fire in 1692 and rebuilt in 1722. In 1935 the Distrito Federal needed more office space, and to maintain the architectural integrity of the Zócalo, the "matching" structure across the street (20 de Noviembre) was built. In 1997, for the first time in 70 years, Mexico City residents were allowed to elect their own mayor (the post had previously been appointed by the president). Thus did the city's first leftist mayor, Cuauhtémoc Cárdenas—son of Mexico's populist president Lázaro Cárdenas—take over the reins in these buildings until 2000.

the zócalo and alameda central

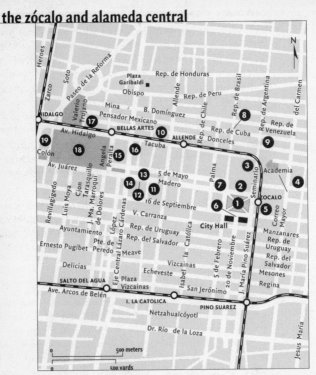

② CATEDRAL METROPOLITANA (Metropolitan Cathedral). Construction on this oldest and largest cathedral in Latin America began in 1573 on the north side of the Zócalo and continued intermittently throughout the next three centuries. The result is a medley of Baroque and neoclassical touches. Inside are four identical domes, their airiness grounded by rows of supportive columns. There are five altars and 14 chapels, mostly in the fussy churrigueresque style, an ornate Baroque style named for Spanish architect José Churriguera (d. 1725). Like most Mexican churches, the cathedral itself is all but overwhelmed by the innumerable paintings, altarpieces, and statues—in graphic color—of Christ and the saints. Over the centuries, this cathedral has sunk noticeably into the spongy subsoil. Its list is evident when viewed from across the square, and engineering projects to stabilize the structure are constantly under way.

② MONTE DE PIEDAD (Mountain of Pity). Now housing the National Pawn Shop—which sells jewelry, antiques, and other goods not reclaimed by their owners—this structure was built to help the poor in the late 18th century. It's on the northwest corner of the Zócalo, on what was once the site of an Aztec palace. *tel. 5/278–1800. Mon.–Sat. about 10–7.*

④ MUSEO JOSÉ LUIS CUEVAS. One of the newest museums downtown, installed in a refurbished former convent, it has a superb collection of contemporary art, as well as work by Mexico's enfant terrible, José Luis Cuevas, who is one of the country's best contemporary artists. Don't miss the sensational *La Giganta* (*The Giantess*), Cuevas's 8-ton bronze sculpture in the central patio. Up-and-coming Latin American artists appear in temporary exhibits throughout the year. *Academia 13, tel. 5/542–8959. 80¢, free Sun. Tues.–Sun. 10–5:30.*

★ **⑤ PALACIO NACIONAL** (National Palace). This grand government building was initiated by Cortés on the site of Moctezuma's home and remodeled by the viceroys. Its current form dates from 1693, although a third floor was added in 1926. Now the seat of government, it has always served as a public-function site. In fact, during colonial times, the first bullfight in New Spain took place in the inner courtyard.

Diego Rivera's sweeping, epic murals on the second floor of the main courtyard have the power to mesmerize. For more than 16 years (1929–45), he and his assistants mounted scaffolds day and night, perfecting techniques adapted from Renaissance Italian frescoes. The result, nearly 1,200 square ft of vividly painted wall space, is grandiosely entitled *Epic of the Mexican People in Their Struggle for Freedom and Independence*. The larger-than-life paintings represent two millennia of Mexican history, filtered through Rivera's imagination. He painted pre-Hispanic times in innocent, almost sugary scenes of Tenochtitlán. Only a few vignettes—a lascivious woman baring her leg in the marketplace, a man offering a human arm for sale, and the carnage of warriors—acknowledge the darker aspects of ancient life. As you walk around the floor, you'll pass images of the savagery of the conquest and the hypocrisy of the Spanish priests, the noble independence movement, and the bloody revolution. Marx appears amid scenes of class struggle, toiling workers, industrialization (which Rivera idealized), bourgeois decadence, and nuclear holocaust. These are among Rivera's finest—as well as most accessible and likely most visited—paintings. The palace also houses two minor museums—dealing with 19th-century president Benito Juárez and the Mexican Congress. And the liberty bell rung by Padre Hidalgo to proclaim independence in 1810 hangs high on the central facade. It chimes every eve of September 16, while from the balcony the president repeats the historic shout of independence to throngs of *chilangos* (Mexico City residents) below. Usually the people demand that the chief executive continue shouting until he loses his voice. *East side of the Zócalo. Free (you will be asked to leave an I.D. at the front desk). Daily 9–5.*

⑧ PLAZA DE SANTO DOMINGO (Santo Domingo Plaza). The Aztec emperor Cuauhtémoc built a palace here, where heretics were later burned at the stake in the Spanish Inquisition. The plaza was the intellectual hub of the city during the colonial era. Today, its most colorful feature is the **Portal de los Evangelistas** (Portal of the Evangelists), filled with scribes at old-fashioned typewriters who are most likely composing letters for love-stricken swains. This age-old custom, which originated when quill pens were in vogue, has successfully launched quite a few of Cupid's arrows. The gloomy-looking **Palace of the Inquisition,** founded by the Catholic Church in 1571 (50 years after the conquest) and closed by government decree in 1820, is catercorner to the lively portal. It was a medical school for many years and now serves as a museum portraying the history of both the Inquisition and medicine. The 18th-century Baroque **Santo Domingo church,** slightly north of the portal, is all that remains of the first Dominican convent in New Spain. The convent building was demolished in 1861 under the Reform laws that forced clerics to turn over all religious buildings not used for worship to the government. Today, you can still see white-robed Dominican nuns visiting the church. *Between República de Cuba, República de Brasil, República de Venezuela, and Palma.*

❸ TEMPLO MAYOR (Great Temple). The ruins of the ancient hub of the Aztec empire were unearthed accidentally in 1978 by telephone repairmen and have since been turned into a vast and historically significant archaeological site and museum. At this temple, dedicated to the Aztec cult of death, captives from rival tribes—as many as 10,000 at a time—were sacrificed to the bloodthirsty god of war, Huitzilopochtli. Seven rows of leering stone skulls adorn one side of the structure.

The adjacent **Museo del Templo Mayor** contains 3,000 pieces unearthed from the site and from other ruins in central Mexico; they include ceramic warriors, stone carvings and knives, skulls of sacrificial victims, a rare gold ingot, models and scale reproductions, and a room on the Spaniards' destruction of Tenochtitlán. The centerpiece is an 8-ton disk discovered at the Templo Mayor. It depicts the moon goddess Coyolxauhqui, who, according to myth, was decapitated and dismembered by her brother Huitzilopochtli for trying to persuade her 400 other brothers to murder their mother. *Seminario 8, at República de Guatemala (entrance on plaza, near Catedral Metropolitana), tel. 5/542–4784, 5/542–4785, 5/542–4786. $2.50, free Sun. Tues.–Sun. 9–5. Call 2 wks ahead to schedule free English-language tours by museum staff, or hire a freelance guide outside the museum.*

❶ **ZÓCALO** (formal name: Plaza de la Constitución). Mexico City's historic plaza and the buildings around it were built by the Spaniards, using Indian slave labor. This enormous paved square, the largest in the Western Hemisphere, occupies the site of the ceremonial center of Tenochtitlán, the capital of the Aztec empire, which once comprised 78 buildings. Throughout the 16th, 17th, and 18th centuries, the Spaniards and their descendants constructed elaborate churches and convents, elegant mansions, and stately public edifices, many of which have long since been converted to other uses. There is an air of Old Europe in this part of the city, which, in its entirety (the Centro Histórico), is a national monument that has been undergoing major refurbishing. Imposing buildings are constructed with the pink volcanic tezontle stone and the quarry stones that the Spaniards recycled from the rubble of the Aztec temples they razed. Throngs of small shops, eateries, cantinas, street vendors, and women in native Indian dress contribute to an inimitably Mexican flavor and exuberance.

Zócalo literally means "pedestal" or "base": in the mid-19th century, an independence monument was planned for the square, but it was never built. The term stuck, however, and now the word "zócalo" is applied to the main plazas of most Mexican cities. Mexico City's Zócalo (because it's the original, it is always capitalized) is used for government rallies, protest marches, sit-ins, and festive events. It is the focal point for Independence Day celebrations on the eve of September 16 and is spectacularly festooned during the Christmas season. Flag-raising and -lowering ceremonies take place here in the early morning and late afternoon. *Bounded on the south by 16 de Septiembre, north by 5 de Mayo, east by Pino Suárez, and west by Monte de Piedad.*

ALAMEDA CENTRAL

⑱ ALAMEDA CENTRAL (Alameda Park). This has been one of the capital's oases of greenery and centers of activity since Aztec times, when the Indians held their *tianguis* (market) on the site. In the early days of the Viceroyalty, the Inquisition burned its victims at the stake here. Later, national leaders, from 18th-century viceroys to Emperor Maximilian and President Porfirio Díaz, clearly envisioned the park as a symbol of civic pride and prosperity: over the centuries, it has been endowed with fountains, railings, a Moorish kiosk imported from Paris, and ash, willow, and poplar trees. Its most conspicuous man-made structure is the semicircular, white marble **Hemiciclo a Benito Juárez** (monument to Juárez) on the Avenida Juárez side of the park. It is a fine place for strolling, relaxing, and listening to live music on Sunday and holidays.

⑬ CASA DE LOS AZULEJOS (House of Tiles). Built as the palace of the counts of the Valle de Orizaba, an aristocratic family from the early period of Spanish rule, this 17th-century masterpiece acquired its name from the tilework installed by a later descendant, a ne'er-do-well scion who married a rich woman. In addition to its well-preserved white, blue, and yellow tiles, the facade also has iron grillwork balconies and gray stonework. One of the prettiest Baroque structures in the country, it is currently occupied by Sanborns, a chain store–restaurant. The dazzling interior, which includes a Moorish patio, a monumental staircase, and a mural by Orozco, is worth seeing. If you have plenty of time—service is slow—this is a good place to stop for breakfast, lunch, or dinner. *Calle Madero 4, at Callejón de la Condesa,*

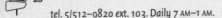

tel. 5/512–9820 ext. 103. Daily 7 AM–1 AM.

⑨ CONJUNTO DE SAN IDELFONSO (San Idelfonso Complex). This colonial building with lovely patios started out as a Jesuit school for the sons of wealthy Mexicans in the 18th century, then took life as a medical college, and finally became a public preparatory school. After a complete renovation, it reopened in 1992 with "Splendors of Mexico: 30 Centuries of Art" and has been showcasing outstanding traveling Mexican exhibits ever since. The interior contains extraordinary works by the big three of mural painting—Diego Rivera, David Alfaro Siqueiros, and Clemente Orozco. *Justo Sierra 16, almost at the corner of República de Argentina, 2 blocks north of Zócalo, tel. 5/789–2505. $2.50, free Tues. Tues.–Sun. 10–6, Wed. and Sat. 10–9.*

⑯ DIRECCIÓN GENERAL DE CORREOS (General Post Office). Mexico City's main post-office building is a fine example of Renaissance revival architecture. Constructed of cream-color sandstone in 1908, it epitomizes the grand imitations of European architecture common in Mexico during the Porfiriato—the rather long dictatorship of Porfirio Díaz (1876–1911). Upstairs, the **Museo del Palacio Postal** shows Mexico's postal history. *Calle Tacuba and Eje Central Lázaro Cárdenas, tel. Museum 5/510–2999, post office 5/521–7394. Free. Museum weekdays 9–4, weekends 10–2; post office weekdays 8–8, Sat. 9–1.*

⑫ IGLESIA DE SAN FRANCISCO. Supposedly the site of Moctezuma's zoo, and certifiably built on the site of Mexico's first convent (1524), this iglesia's current 18th-century French Gothic incarnation is one of the newest buildings on the street. The paintings inside are beautiful. *Calles Madero and 16 de Septiembre, tel. no phone. Daily 7 AM–8:30 PM.*

⑰ MUSEO FRANZ MAYER. Opened in 1986 in the 16th-century Hospital de San Juan de Dios, this museum has exhibits that include 16th- and 17th-century antiques, such as wooden chests inlaid with ivory, tortoiseshell, and ebony; tapestries, paintings, and lacquerware; rococo clocks, glassware, and architectural ornamentation; and an unusually large assortment of Talavera ceramics and *azulejos*, or tiles. The museum also has an impressive collection of more than 700 editions of Cervantes's *Don Quixote*. The old hospital building is faithfully restored, with pieces of the original frescoes peeking through. *Av. Hidalgo 45, at Plaza Santa Veracruz, tel. 5/518–2267. $1.50, free Tues. Tues.–Sun. 10–5. Call 1 day ahead for an English-speaking guide.*

⑲ MUSEO MURAL DIEGO RIVERA. Diego Rivera's controversial mural, *Sunday Afternoon Dream in the Alameda Park*, originally was painted on a lobby wall of the Hotel Del Prado in 1947–48. Its controversy grew out of Rivera's Marxist inscription, "God does not exist," which the artist later replaced with the bland "Conference of San Juan de Letrán" to placate Mexico's dominant Catholic population. The 1985 earthquake destroyed the hotel but not the poetic mural. This museum was built across the street from the hotel to house the work. *Calles Balderas and Colón, tel. 5/510–2329. $1, free Sun. Tues.–Sun. 10–6.*

⑩ MUSEO NACIONAL DE ARTE (National Art Museum). This neoclassical building, built during the Porfiriato and turned into a museum in 1982, contains a superb collection from nearly every school of Mexican art, with a concentration on Mexico's artistic development from 1810 to 1950. The museum was undergoing restoration in 2000 and scheduled to reopen by October 2000. Works include Diego Rivera's portrait of Adolfo Best Maugard, José María Velasco's *Vista del Valle de México desde el Cerro de Santa Isabel* (*View of the Valley of Mexico from the Hill of Santa Isabel*), and Ramón Cano Manilla's *El Globo* (*The Balloon*). *El Caballito*, a statue of Spain's Carlos V on horseback, stands out front. *Calle Tacuba 8, tel. 5/512–3224. $2, free Sun. Tues.–Sun. 10–5:30.*

★ ⑮ PALACIO DE BELLAS ARTES (Fine Arts Palace). Construction on this colossal white-marble opera house was begun in 1904 by Porfirio Díaz, who wanted to add yet another ornamental building to his accomplishments. He was ousted seven years later after winning yet another rigged election. He died in 1915, and the building wasn't finished until 1934. Today the theater serves as a handsome venue for international and national artists, including such groups as the Ballet Folklórico de México (☞ The Arts in Nightlife and the Arts). The palace is indeed renowned for its architecture, the work of Italian Adamo Boari, who also designed the post office; it includes an art-nouveau facade trimmed in pre-Hispanic motifs. Inside are a Tiffany stained-glass curtain depicting the two volcanoes outside Mexico City and paintings by several celebrated Mexican artists, including Rufino Tamayo and Mexico's trio of muralists: Rivera, Orozco, and Siqueiros. Temporary art exhibits are also held here. *Eje Central Lázaro Cárdenas and Av. Juárez, tel. 5/512–3633. $2.50 for exhibits, free Sun. (no charge to look at the building and gift shops inside). Building Tues.–Sun. 10–9, exhibits Tues.–Sun. 10–5:30.*

OFF THE BEATEN PATH   **TLATELOLCO** – At Avenida Reforma's northern end, about 2 km (1 mi) north of the Palacio de Bellas Artes, the area known as Tlatelolco (pronounced tla-tel-ohl-coh) was the domain of Cuauhtémoc (pronounced kwa-oo-teh-muck)—the last Aztec emperor before the conquest—and the sister city of Tenochtitlán. In modern times its name makes residents shudder, because it was here that the Mexican army massacred several hundred protesting students in 1968. In addition, the 1985 earthquake destroyed several high-rise apartments in Tlatelolco, killing hundreds. The center of Tlatelolco is the **Plaza de las Tres Culturas,** so named because Mexico's three cultural eras—pre-Hispanic, colonial, and modern—are represented on the plaza in the form of the small ruins of a pre-Hispanic ceremonial center (visible from the roadway); the Iglesia de Santiago Tlatelolco (1609) and Colegio de la Santa Cruz de Tlatelolco (1535–36); and the ultracontemporary Ministry of Foreign Affairs (1970). The *colegio* (college), founded by the Franciscans after the conquest, was once attended by the sons of the Aztec nobility. *Plaza is bounded on the north by Manuel González, on the west by Av. San Juan de Letrán Nte., and on the east by Paseo de la Reforma, between Glorietas de Peralvillo and Cuitláhuac.*

⑪ **PALACIO DE ITURBIDE** (Emperor Iturbide's Palace). Built in 1780, this handsome Baroque structure—note the imposing door and its carved-stone trimmings—became the residence of Iturbide in 1822. One of the heroes of the independence movement, the misguided Iturbide proclaimed himself emperor of a country that had thrown off the imperial yoke of the Hapsburgs only a year before. His own empire, needless to say, was short-lived. Now his home is owned by Banamex (Banco Nacional de México) and sponsors cultural exhibits in the atrium. *Calle Madero 17, tel. 5/225–0281. Free. Inner atrium daily 9–3.*

⑭ **TORRE LATINOAMERICANA** (Latin American Tower). Touted as the tallest building in the capital before the Hotel de Mexico was built in the 1980s, this 47-story skyscraper was completed in 1956, and on clear days the observation deck and café on the top floors afford fine views of the city. The **Fantastic World of the Sea,** a sky-high aquarium, miraculously transported small sharks and crocodiles to the 38th floor. *Calle Madero and Eje Central Lázaro Cárdenas, tel. Observation deck 5/521–0844, aquarium 5/521–7455. Deck $3.20, aquarium $2.20. Deck daily 9:30 AM–11 PM; aquarium daily 9:30 AM–10 PM.*

ZONA ROSA, BOSQUE DE CHAPULTEPEC, AND COLONIA CONDESA

Bosque de Chapultepec, originally called Cerro de Chapultepec, is the largest park in the city, a great green refuge from gray urban living. Housing five world-class museums, a castle, a lake, an amusement park, and the Mexican president's official residence, Chapultepec is a saving grace for visitors and locals. Be sure to visit the Museo Nacional de Antropología—

you won't find the likes of its exhibits anywhere else.

The Zona Rosa, once a cultural center of Mexico City, is now a first stop for shopping, where stores, hotels, travel agencies, and restaurants line the avenues. Nearby Colonia Condesa is the newcomer on foreigners' itineraries. This tranquil neighborhood is filled with casual cafés and the city's hottest new eateries.

Emperor Maximilian built the Paseo de la Reforma in 1865, modeling it after the Champs-Élysées in Paris. Its purpose was to connect the Palacio Nacional (☞ Sights to See in Zócalo and Alameda Central, *above*) with his residence, the Castillo de Chapultepec. At the northern end of Reforma are Tlatelolco (☞ Sights to See in Zócalo and Alameda Central, *above*), the Lagunilla Market, and Plaza Garibaldi, where the mariachis gather. To the south, Reforma winds its leisurely way west into the wealthy neighborhoods of Lomas de Chapultepec, where most of the houses and estates sit behind stone walls.

Sights to See

BOSQUE DE CHAPULTEPEC

㉑ **BOSQUE DE CHAPULTEPEC** ("The Woods of Chapultepec," or Chapultepec Park). This 1,600-acre green space, divided into three sections, draws families on weekend outings, cyclists, and joggers. And its museums—including the Museo Nacional de Antropología—are among the finest in Mexico. This is one of the oldest parts of Mexico City, having been inhabited by the Mexica (Aztec) tribe as early as the 13th century. The Mexica poet-king Nezahualcoyotl had his palace here and ordered construction of the aqueduct that brought water to Tenochtitlán. Ahuehuete trees (Moctezuma cypress) still stand from that era, when the woods were used as hunting preserves.

At the park's principal entrance, one block west of the Chapultepec metro station, the **Monumento a los Niños Héroes** (Monument to the Boy Heroes) consists of six marble columns adorned with eaglets. Supposedly buried in the monument are the six young cadets who wrapped themselves in the Mexican flag and jumped to their deaths rather than surrender to the Americans during the U.S. invasion of 1847. To Mexicans, that war is still a troubling symbol of their neighbor's aggressive dominance: the war cost Mexico almost half of its national territory—the present states of Texas, California, Arizona, New Mexico, and Nevada.

Other sights in the first section of Bosque de Chapultepec include three small boating lakes, a botanical garden, and the Casa del Lago cultural center, which hosts free plays, cultural events, and live music on weekends. **Los Pinos,** the residential palace of the president of Mexico, is on a small highway called Avenida Constituyentes, which cuts through the park. This is heavily guarded and cannot be visited.

The less-crowded second and third sections of Bosque de Chapultepec contain a fancy restaurant; ☞ **La Feria de Chapultepec;** ☞ **El Papalote, Museo del Niño**; the national cemetery; and the *Lienzo Charro* (Mexican rodeos) held on Sunday afternoon.

★ ㉒ **CASTILLO DE CHAPULTEPEC** (Chapultepec Castle). On Cerro del Chapulín (Grasshopper Hill), the Castillo has borne witness to all the turbulence and grandeur of Mexican history. In its earliest permutations, it was a Mexica palace, where the Indians made one of their last stands against the Spaniards. Later it was a Spanish hermitage, gunpowder plant, and military college. Emperor Maximilian used the castle, parts of which date from 1783, as his residence, and his example was followed by various presidents from 1872 to 1940, when Lázaro Cárdenas decreed that it be turned into the **Museo Nacional de Historia** (National History Museum).

Displays on the museum's ground floor cover Mexican history from the conquest to the revolution. The bathroom, bedroom, tea salon, and gardens were used by Maximilian and his wife,

Av. Ejército Nacional
Newton
Av. Ejército Nacional
B. Sta. Barbara
Av. Parque Via
Arquimedes
Av. Thiers
Villalongín
R. Sena
POLANCO
Av.
Horacio
Gutenberg
Río Tíber
Rhin
POLANCO
Calz. Mariano Escobedo
Río
Guadalquivir
Río
i Tourist Office
Calz. Ruben Darío
Calz. Melchor Ocampo
Calz. M. Gandhi
R. Lerma
Paseo de la Reforma
20
ZONA ROSA
Calz. Chivatito
AUDITORIO
26
25
Paseo de la Reforma
SEVILLA
27
24
Bosque de Chapultepec
CHAPULTEPEC
Av. Chapultepec
22 23
Av. Sonora
Av. Caxaca
Veracruz
Av. Durango
Calz. Jose Vasconselos
21
CONDESA
Av. Obregón
Presidential Palace
Eje 2 Sur
JUANACATLAN
28 Laredo
Mazatlán
CONSTITUYENTES
Michoacán
Cuernavaca
Soho
El Pendulo
Sur
Manzanillo
Tamaulipas
Citlaltepetl
Av. Insurgentes

0 ——— 550 yards
0 ——— 500 meters

Carlotta, during the 19th century. The ground floor also contains works by 20th-century muralists O'Gorman, Orozco, and Siqueiros, while the upper floor is devoted to temporary exhibits, Porfirio Díaz's malachite vases, and religious art. A 30¢ shuttle bus runs between this museum and the Museo del Caracol. *Section 1 of Bosque de Chapultepec, tel. 5/553–6224, 5/286–9920. $2, free Sun. Tues.–Sun. 9–5.*

🐾 **LA FERIA DE CHAPULTEPEC.** This children's amusement park has various games and more than 50 rides, including a truly hair-raising haunted house and a *montaña rusa*—"Russian mountain," or roller coaster. *Section 2 of Bosque de Chapultepec, tel. 5/230–2112. $7.50 day pass includes all rides. Tues.–Fri. 11–7, weekends 10–9.*

★ **㉔ MUSEO DE ARTE MODERNO** (Museum of Modern Art). Exhibits here focus on Mexican artists. One room is devoted to Mexican plastic arts from the 1930s to the 1960s; four other rooms feature revolving exhibits of contemporary painters, sculptors, lithographers, and photographers from around the world. *Paseo de la Reforma and Calle Gandhi, Section 1 of Bosque de Chapultepec, tel. 5/553–6313. $1.50, free Sun. Tues.–Sun. 10–6.*

🐾 **㉓ MUSEO DEL CARACOL.** Officially it's the Galería de la Lucha del Pueblo Mexicano por su Libertad, but most people refer to it by the more fanciful name Museum of the Snail because of its spiral shape. The gallery concentrates on the 400 years from the establishment of the Viceroyalty to the Constitution of 1917, using dioramas and light-and-sound displays that children can appreciate. *Section 1 of Bosque de Chapultepec, on the ramp up to the Castillo, tel. 5/553–6285. $2. Tues.–Sun. 9–5:30.*

★ **㉖ MUSEO NACIONAL DE ANTROPOLOGÍA** (National Museum of Anthropology). This is the greatest museum in the country—and arguably one of the finest archaeological museums anywhere. Even its architectural design, by Pedro Ramírez Vázquez, is distinguished. The museum is arranged on two floors, surrounded by salons, each displaying artifacts from a particular geographic region and/or culture. The collection is so extensive—covering some 100,000 square ft—that you could easily spend a day here, and that might be barely adequate. Labels and explanations are in Spanish, but you can reserve and hire (for about $70 for up to 20 people) an English-speaking tour guide by calling the museum one week in advance, or hire an unofficial bilingual guide outside the museum for about $10. The museum has English audio guides for rent for $3.50, and English-language guidebooks are available in the bookshop.

A good place to start is in the Orientation Room, where a film is shown in Spanish nearly every hour on the hour during the week and every two hours on the weekends. The film traces the course of Mexican prehistory and the pre-Hispanic cultures of Mesoamerica. The 12 ground-floor rooms treat pre-Hispanic cultures by region—such as Sala Teotihuacána, Sala Tolteca, Sala Oaxaca (Zapotec and Mixtec peoples), Sala Maya (Maya groups from many areas, including Guatemala), and so on. The famous Aztec calendar stone, the original *Piedra del Sol* (Stone of the Sun) is found in Room 7, the Sala Mexica, which describes Aztec life. A copy of the Aztec ruler Moctezuma's feathered headdress is displayed nearby in the same salon—strangely, the original headdress is in Vienna. An original stela from Tula, near Mexico City, massive Olmec heads from Veracruz, and vivid reproductions of Maya murals in a reconstructed temple are some of the other highlights. The magnificent tomb of the 8th-century Maya ruler Pacal, which was discovered in the ruins of Palenque, is another must to explore (Sala Maya). The perfectly preserved skeletal remains lie in state in an immense stone chamber, and the stairwell walls leading to it are beautifully decorated with bas-relief scenes of the underworld. Pacal's jade death mask is also on display nearby. The ground floor is filled with everything from the early remnants of nomadic societies to the statuary, jewelry, weapons, figurines, and pottery that evoke the brilliant, quirky, and frequently bloodthirsty civilizations that peopled Mesoamerica for the 3,000 years that preceded the Spanish invasion.

The nine rooms on the upper floor contain faithful ethnographic displays of current indigenous peoples, using maps, photographs, household objects, folk art, clothing, and religious articles. When leaving the museum, take a rest and watch the famous Voladores de Papantla (flyers of Papantla) as they swing by their feet down an incredibly high maypolelike structure. *Paseo de la Reforma at Calle Gandhi, Section 1 of Bosque de Chapultepec, tel. 5/286–2923, 5/553–6381, 5/553–6386 for a guide. $2.50, free Sun. Tues.–Sun. 9–7.*

★ **㉕ MUSEO RUFINO TAMAYO** (Rufino Tamayo Museum). Within its modernist shell, this sleek museum contains the paintings of the noted Mexican muralist, works from his private collection, and temporary exhibits of pieces by contemporary artists from around the world. The majority of paintings are by Tamayo; those from his collection, which demonstrate his unerring eye for great art, include a Picasso and a few works by Joan Miró, René Magritte, Francis Bacon, and Henry Moore. *Paseo de la Reforma at Calle Gandhi, Section 1 of Bosque de Chapultepec, tel. 5/286–6519. $1.50, free Sun. Tues.–Sun. 10–6.*

☙ **EL PAPALOTE, MUSEO DEL NIÑO** (The Butterfly, Children's Museum). Five theme sections compose this excellent interactive museum: *Our World*; *The Human Body*; the pun-intended *Con-Sciencia*, with exhibits relating to both consciousness and science; *Communication*, on topics ranging from language to computers; and *Expression*, which includes art, music, theater, and literature. There are also workshops, an IMAX theater, a store, and a restaurant. *Av. Constituyentes 268, Section 2 of Bosque de Chapultepec, tel. 5/237–1781. $4. Weekdays 9–1 and 2–6; weekends 10–2 and 3–7.*

☙ **RIPLEY'S MUSEO DE LO INCREÍBLE** (Ripley's Museum of the Incredible) and the **Museo de Cera de la Ciudad de Mexico** (Mexico City Wax Museum). Although these museums lack the polish of their equivalents in, say, New York, they are nonetheless fun for children of all ages. The Ripley's museum has 14 exhibit rooms chockablock with believe-it-or-not items, and in the wax museum, Placido Domingo and Mexican politicians come to life. *Londres 4 (east of Zona Rosa), tel. 5/546–3784. $3 each museum or $4 for both. Weekdays 11–7, weekends 10–7.*

27 **ZOOLÓGICO.** During the early 16th century, Mexico City's zoo housed a small private collection of animals belonging to Moctezuma II; it became quasi-public when he allowed favored subjects to visit it. The current zoo opened on this site in the 1920s and has the usual suspects as well as some superstar pandas. A gift from China, the original pair—Pepe and Ying Ying—produced the world's first panda baby born in captivity (much to competitive China's chagrin). The zoo also produced the first spectacled bears in captivity in 1998, the same year officials added the Moctezuma Aviary. The zoo is surrounded by a miniature train depot, botanical gardens, and lakes where you can go rowing. You'll see the entrance on Paseo de la Reforma, across from the Museo Nacional de Antropología. *Section 1 of Bosque de Chapultepec, tel. 5/553–6263, 5/256–4104. Free; English audio guide $2.50. Tues.–Sun. 9:30–4:15.*

COLONIA CONDESA

28 **COLONIA CONDESA.** The neighborhood sprang up in the early 1900s around the city's elite, who quickly abandoned it in the '40s for other more-fashionable areas, leaving decaying mansions and parks behind. Today, the neighborhood is getting renovation from an influx of new residents, mostly young artists, entrepreneurs, and foreigners. Restaurants have sprung up everywhere in the colonia, quickly making Condesa a new center for cuisine.

Condesa doesn't have much in the way of museums or monuments, but it is the perfect place to break from a hectic day of sightseeing—just sit back in one of the neighborhood's relaxed sidewalk cafés and watch Mexico go by. And with a new restaurant opening nearly every week, it is the place to come for dinner. The main drag is Avenida Michoacán, from which restaurants radiate out in every direction. Avenida México loops the main park in the area, Parque México, and Avenida Amsterdam makes another loop around the area. The park area used to be a racetrack, which explains the looping roads.

There is also an abundance of hip and trendy clothing shops in the area. The most famous are on Michoacán: Soho (tel. 5/553–1730), for example, is a clothing and music store whose name refers to the often-made comparison of Condesa to New York's Soho neighborhood in the 1950s; the trendy La Esquina clothing store (tel. 5/211–2951) down the street is similar. Another great shop to browse through is El Péndulo (Nuevo León 115, tel. 5/286–9493), a sort of cultural center. It has a large selection of Spanish books and an international collection of CDs, and the restaurant has a great breakfast menu, with classical guitarists playing on Sunday morning. El Péndulo often hosts other performers—jazz, classical, folk, or rock bands—on weekends.

Farther east on Michoacán, you can head to the Parque México or the smaller Parque España for a picnic or a stroll. There's a great movie theater right on the Parque España that shows Hollywood and Mexican films, the Plaza Condesa (tel. 5/286–4973); it has waiters who will serve you popcorn and drinks during the flick. From Michoacán, take Tamaulipas north about four blocks to arrive at the park and theater.

ZONA ROSA

For years the Zona Rosa has been a favorite part of the city because of its plethora of restaurants, cafés, art and antiques galleries, hotels, discos, and shops. With the mushrooming of fast-food places and some tacky bars and stores, the Zona—as it is affectionately called—has lost some of its former gloss, but nonetheless still draws the faithful. Most of the buildings in the

Zona Rosa are on a very human scale, at two or three stories high: they were originally private homes built in the 1920s for the wealthy. All the streets are wistfully named after European cities; some, such as Génova, are garden-lined pedestrian malls accented with contemporary bronze statuary.

To enjoy the Zona Rosa, just walk the lengths of Hamburgo and Londres and some of the side streets, especially Copenhague—a veritable restaurant row. The large crafts market on Londres is officially Mercado Insurgentes, although most people call it either Mercado Zona Rosa or Mercado Londres. Just opposite the market's Londres entrance is Plaza del Angel, a small upscale shopping mall, the halls of which are crowded by antiques vendors on weekends.

㉒ MONUMENTO A LA INDEPENDENCIA (Independence Monument). A Corinthian column topped by a gold-covered angel is the city's most beautiful monument, built to celebrate the 100th anniversary of Mexico's War of Independence. Beneath the pedestal lie the remains of the principal heroes of the independence movement; an eternal flame burns in their honor. *Traffic circle between Calle Río Tiber, Paseo de la Reforma, and Calle Florencia.*

SAN ANGEL AND COYOACÁN

Originally separate colonial towns, San Angel and Coyoacán were both absorbed by the ever-growing capital. In the process they've managed to retain their original pueblo charm and tranquility.

San Angel is a little colonial enclave of cobblestone streets, stone walls, pastel houses, and gardens drenched in bougainvillea. It became a haven for wealthy Spaniards during the Viceroyalty period, around the time of the construction of the Ex-Convento del Carmen. The elite were drawn to the area because of its rivers, pleasant climate, and rural ambience, and proceeded to build haciendas and mansions that, for many, were country homes. Like neighboring Coyoacán, San Angel was just a suburb of Mexico City until the government decided to incorporate it into the capital.

Coyoacán means "Place of the Coyotes." According to local legend, a coyote used to bring chickens to a friar who had saved the coyote from being strangled by a snake. Coyoacán was founded by Toltecs in the 10th century and later settled by the Aztecs, or Mexica. Bernal Díaz Castillo, a Spanish chronicler, wrote that there were 6,000 houses at the time of the conquest. Cortés set up headquarters in Coyoacán during his siege of Tenochtitlán and at one point considered making it his capital. He changed his mind for political reasons, but many of the Spanish buildings left from the two-year period during which Mexico City was built still stand.

Coyoacán has had many illustrious residents from Mexico's rich and intellectual elite, including Miguel de la Madrid, president of Mexico from 1982 to 1988; artists Frida Kahlo, Diego Rivera, and José Clemente Orozco; Gabriel Figueroa, cinematographer for Luis Buñuel and John Huston; film star Dolores del Río; film director El Indio Fernández; and writers Carlos Monsiváis, Elena Poniatowska, and Jorge Ibargüengoitia. It is also the neighborhood where Leon Trotsky in exile met his violent death. Although superficially it resembles San Angel, Coyoacán has a more animated street life. Most of the houses and other buildings honor the traditions of colonial Mexican architecture, and the neighborhood is well kept by residents, many of whose families have lived here for generations.

Sights to See

SAN ANGEL

③ **CASA DEL RISCO** (Risco House). This 1681 mansion is one of the prettiest houses facing the Plaza San Jacinto. A huge free-form fountain sculpture—exploding with colorful porcelain, tiles, shells, and mosaics—covers the entire eastern wall of its patio. Although it's not ranked among the city's top museums, the

san angel and coyoacán

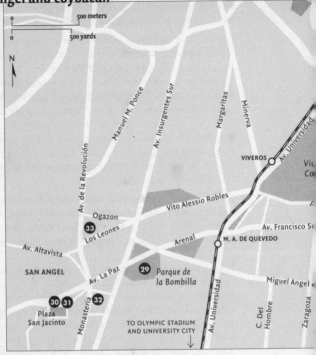

0 ——— 500 meters
0 ——— 500 yards

N

Manuel M. Ponce
Av. Insurgentes Sur
Margaritas
Minerva
Av. de la Revolución
VIVEROS
Av. Universidad
Vil
Co
Vito Alessio Robles
Ogazon
Los Leones **33**
Av. Francisco So
Av. Altavista
Arenal
M. A. DE QUEVEDO
SAN ANGEL
29 Parque de
la Bombilla
Miguel Angel
Av. La Paz **32**
Monasteria
30 **31**
Plaza
San Jacinto
TO OLYMPIC STADIUM
AND UNIVERSITY CITY
Av. Universidad
C. Del
Hombre
Zaragoza

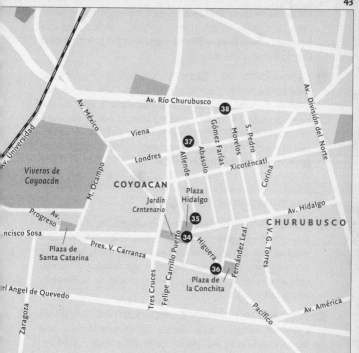

Museo de la Casa del Risco houses a splendid collection of 17th- and 18th-century European and colonial Mexican paintings as well as period furnishings. *Plaza San Jacinto 15, tel. 5/616–2711. Free. Tues.–Sun. 10–5.*

32 **EX-CONVENTO DEL CARMEN** (Carmelite Convent and Church). Erected by Carmelite friars with the help of an Indian chieftain between 1615 and 1628, this cloister, with its tile-covered domes, fountains, and gardens, is one of the most interesting examples of colonial religious architecture in this part of the city. The church still operates, but the convent is now the **Museo Regional del Carmen,** with a fine collection of 16th- to 18th-century religious paintings, icons, and 12 mummified corpses. *Av. Revolución 4, at Monasterio, tel. 5/616–2816, 5/616–1177. $2, free Sun. Tues.–Sun. 10–4:45.*

29 **MONUMENTO AL GENERAL ALVARO OBREGÓN.** This somber gray granite monument marks the spot where reformer and national hero Obregón was gunned down by a religious zealot in a restaurant in 1928, soon before he was to begin his second term as president. *Parque de la Bombilla, east of Av. La Paz at Av. Insurgentes.*

33 **MUSEO ALVAR Y CARMEN T. DE CARRILLO GIL.** This private collection contains early murals by Orozco, Rivera, and Siqueiros; works by modern European artists such as Klee and Picasso; and temporary expositions of young Mexican artists. *Av. Revolución 1608, at Desierto de los Leones, tel. 5/550–1254. $1. Tues.–Sun. 10–6.*

★ **30** **PLAZA SAN JACINTO.** This cozy plaza with a grisly history is the center of San Angel. In 1847 about 50 Irish soldiers of St. Patrick's Battalion, who had sided with the Mexicans in the Mexican-American War, had their foreheads branded here with the letter D—for deserter—and were then hanged by the Americans. These men had been enticed to swim the Rio Grande, deserting the ranks of U.S. General Zachary Taylor, by pleas to the historic and religious ties between Spain and Ireland. As settlers in Mexican Texas, they felt their allegiance lay with Catholic Mexico, and they were among the bravest fighters in the war. They met their end when the American flag flew over Castillo de Chapultepec (☞ Sights to See *in* Zona Rosa, Bosque de Chapultepec, and Colonia Condesa, *above*) after the death of the *niños héroes*. A memorial plaque (on a building on the plaza's west side) lists their names and expresses Mexico's gratitude for their help in the "unjust North American invasion." Off to one side of the plaza, the excellent handicrafts market, Bazar Sábado, is held on Saturday (☞ Markets *in* Shopping). *Between Miramon, Cda. Santisima, Dr. Galvez, and Madero.*

COYOACÁN

㉟ CASA DE CORTÉS (Cortés's House). The place where the Aztec emperor Cuauhtémoc was held prisoner by Cortés is reputed to have been rebuilt in the 18th century from the stones of his original house by one of Cortés's descendants; the municipal government now has offices here. Dominating the little square on which it sits, this was almost the city's first city hall, but Cortés decided to rebuild Tenochtitlán instead. The two-story, deep-red house, with its wide arches and tile patio, is gorgeous. The house is not open to the public, but there is a tourist-information booth in the front room that's staffed by friendly employees eager to tell you about Coyoacán. *Plaza Hidalgo between Calles Carillo Puerto and Caballo Calco.*

㊱ CASA DE LA MALINCHE. One of the most powerful symbols of the conquest is located in Coyoacán but, significantly perhaps, is not even marked. It's the somber-looking, fortresslike residence of Malinche, Cortés's Indian mistress and interpreter, whom the Spaniards called Doña María and the Indians called Malintzín. Malinche aided the conquest by enabling Cortés to communicate with the Nahuatl-speaking tribes he met en route to Tenochtitlán. Today she is a much-reviled Mexican symbol of a traitorous xenophile—hence the term *malinchista*, used to describe a Mexican who prefers things foreign. Legend says that Cortés's wife died in this house, poisoned by the conquistador. *2 blocks east of Plaza Hidalgo on Calle Higuera at Vallarta.*

34 JARDÍN CENTENARIO (Centenary Gardens). Small fairs, amateur musical performances, and poetry and palm readings are frequent occurrences in this large park surrounded by outdoor cafés. At the far end of the Jardín you'll see **Templo de San Juan Bautista,** one of the first churches to be built in New Spain. It was completed in 1582, and its door has a Baroque arch. *Between Calle Centenario, Av. Hidalgo, and Caballo Calco.*

★ **37 MUSEO DE FRIDA KAHLO.** The house where the painter Frida Kahlo was born (in 1907)—and lived with Diego Rivera almost continuously from 1929 until her death in 1954—is fascinating. Kahlo has become a cult figure, not only because of her paintings—55 of 143 are self-portraits—but also because of her bohemian lifestyle and flamboyant individualism. As a child Kahlo was crippled by polio, and several years later she was impaled on a tramway rail. She had countless operations, including the amputation of a leg; was addicted to painkillers; had affairs with Leon Trotsky and several women; and married Rivera twice. Kahlo's astounding vitality and originality are reflected in this house, from the giant papier-mâché skeletons outside and the painted tin *retablos* (ex-votos) on the staircase to the gloriously decorated kitchen and the bric-a-brac in her bedroom. Even if you know nothing about Kahlo, a visit to the museum will leave you with a strong, visceral impression of this pivotal feminist artist. *Londres 247, at Allende, tel. 5/554–5999. $2. Tues.–Sun. 10–5:45.*

38 MUSEO DE LEON TROTSKY. Resembling an anonymous and forbidding fortress, with turrets for armed guards, this is where Leon Trotsky lived and was murdered. It is difficult to believe that it's the final resting place for the ashes of one of the most important figures of the Russian Revolution, but that only adds to the allure of the house, which is owned by Trotsky's grandson.

This is a modest, austere dwelling. Anyone taller than 5 ft must stoop to pass through doorways to Trotsky's bedroom—with bullet holes still in the walls from the first assassination attempt, in which the muralist Siqueiros was implicated—his wife's study, the dining room, and the study where the Mexican communist Ramón Mercader finally drove an ice pick into Trotsky's head. On his desk, cluttered with writing paraphernalia and an article he was revising in Russian, the calendar is open to that fateful day, August 20, 1940. The volunteers will tell you how Trotsky's teeth left a permanent scar on Mercader's hand, how he clung to life for 26 hours, what his last words were, and how his death was sponsored by the United States (others would say Stalin). Not all the volunteers, however, speak English. *Río Churubusco 410, tel. 5/ 658–8732. $1. Tues.–Sun. 10–5.*

🐾 **NUEVO REINO AVENTURA.** This 100-acre theme park on the southern edge of the city comprises seven "villages": Mexican, French, Swiss, Polynesian, Moroccan, the Wild West, and Children's World. Shows include performances by trained dolphins. The most famous of the playful swimmers was an orca whale named Keiko, star of the film *Free Willy*, who was sent to an aquarium in Oregon to recover his health before he was released into his native Icelandic waters in 1998. *Southwest of Coyoacán on Carretera Picacho a Ajusco at Km 1.5, tel. 5/645–5434, 5/ 645–6232. $14 includes entrance and all rides. Tues.–Thurs. 10–6, Fri.–Sun. 10–7.*

In This Chapter

Updated by Patricia Alisau

eating out

MEXICO CITY RESTAURANTS open 7–11 AM for breakfast (*desayuno*), 1–5 for lunch (*comida*), and most locals start out at 9 PM for dinner (*cena*). Restaurants stay open till midnight during the week and a little later on weekends. At deluxe restaurants, dress is generally formal (jacket and tie), and reservations are almost always required; see reviews for details. (Even if a deluxe restaurant doesn't *require* a jacket and tie, men are likely to feel out-of-place if not well dressed.)

Credit cards—especially American Express, MasterCard, and Visa—are widely accepted at pricier restaurants. The bargains are usually cash only.

Colonia Polanco is an attractive, upscale neighborhood on the edge of Chapultepec Park that has some of the best and most expensive dining (and lodging) in the city.

Zona Rosa restaurants get filled pretty quickly on Saturday night, especially the Saturday coinciding with most people's payday, which falls on the 1st and 15th of each month.

CATEGORY	COST*
$$$$	over $40
$$$	$25–$40
$$	$15–$25
$	under $15

*per person for a three-course meal, excluding drinks and service

ARGENTINE

$$$ CAMBALACHE. Before entering this ever-busy beef lover's dream, you can see the chefs preparing their thick cuts in the window. If you come with a few people, try the Super Lomo Cambalache, a steak big enough for three–four people. If you're not in the mood for beef, there are several chicken dishes on the menu, such as the Don Ignacio: a boneless chicken breast served in a mushroom sauce with pineapple and fresh sweet peppers. Vegetables *do* come with menu items, and potatoes, particularly the soufflé, are a specialty. *Arquímedes 85, Col. Polanco, tel. 5/280–2080, 5/280–2957. AE, MC, V.*

$$$ RINCON ARGENTINO. This most talked about Argentine restaurant in the city is known as much for its decor as for its exquisitely prepared cuts of beef. The interior is like the outdoors, with the ceiling painted into a sky, the bar covered by a thatch roof, and the dining areas turned into a stone-and-wood lodge. The focus here is beef—such as *lomo mignon*, filet mignon served with bacon and a rich mushroom sauce. Most Argentines prefer their beef *bien cocida* (well-done), but you can have it any way you like. *Presidente Masarik 177, Col. Polanco, tel. 5/531–8617, 5/254–8775. AE, MC, V.*

$ FONDA GARUFA. Its tables spilling out onto a Condesa sidewalk, this is a perfect place for a relaxed meal after a day of sightseeing. Filet mignon, served with mushrooms and watercress, is especially delicious. There's also an extensive list of innovative pastas. A favorite with regulars is fettuccine Hindú: half a chicken breast bathed in a yogurt sauce laced with cilantro, ginger, onion, and chili, over fresh fettuccine. *Michoacán 93, Col. Condesa, tel. 5/286–8295. AE, MC, V.*

FRENCH

$$$$ FOUQUET'S DE PARIS. In the Camino Real hotel, this branch of
★ the renowned Parisian restaurant is an elegant haven of peace

and tranquility. The best pâtés in Mexico and tender, juicy lamb chops are part of the diverse and stylish menu. Desserts are in a class of their own: sorbets, such as the delicately flavored passion fruit, are outstanding, and the cakes, mousses, and pastries are light and delicious. Monthlong gastronomic festivals are held here throughout the year, and each October or November chefs from the original Fouquet's in Paris take over the kitchen. *Hotel Camino Real, Mariano Escobedo 700, Col. Polanco, tel. 5/203–2121. Reservations essential. Jacket and tie. AE, DC, MC, V. Closed Sun. No lunch Sat.*

$$$ CHAMPS ÉLYSÉES. Commanding a superb view of the
★ Independence Monument is one of the bastions of haute cuisine in Mexico City. The variety of sauces served with both meat and fish dishes is impressive—hollandaise over sea bass or red snapper takes top honors. Regulars find either the roast duck (carved at your table) or the classic pepper steak hard to resist. The cheese board is particularly generous. *Paseo de la Reforma 316, at Estocolmo, Zona Rosa, tel. 5/525–7259. AE, DC, MC, V. Closed Sun.*

$ EL BUEN COMER. One of the more original Polanco eating spots, El Buen Comer (which means "eating well") consists of not more than 20 tables in the covered garage of a private house. The entrance is easily missed, and the atmosphere inside is that of a large, private lunch party. The emphasis is on French cuisine from Lyon. House specialties include an endive salad with a cream-and-nut vinaigrette served with scallops. The fondues and pâtés are excellent. The quiche royale with shrimp is a must for seafood lovers. Desserts include mango or chocolate mousse or raspberries smothered in cream. El Buen Comer makes a great stop after shopping in Polanco. *Edgar Allan Poe 50, Col. Polanco, tel. 5/282–0325. Reservations essential. AE, MC, V. Closed Sun. No dinner.*

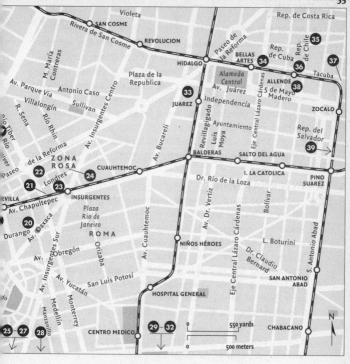

GREEK

$ AGAPI MU (My Love). This 16-table Greek bistro tucked in a converted Colonia Condesa home with a Greek flag out front and snug rooms inside attracts its share of actors, singers, and artists. Come for authentic Greek food in a casual, intimate setting and rambunctious Greek song and dance Thursday through Saturday nights. The menu includes *paputsáka* (stuffed eggplant), *kalamárea* (fried squid Greek style), and *dolmádes* (stuffed grape leaves). Wash it all down with a Hungarian Sangre de Toro wine, and finish it off with a smooth, sweet Greek coffee. *Alfonso Reyes 96, Col. Condesa, tel. 5/286–1384. AE, MC, V.*

INTERNATIONAL

$$$$ MAXIM'S DE PARIS. Under the auspices of the original Parisian Maxim's, this spacious but intimate Art Deco restaurant sits under a stained-glass ceiling and serves classic Gallic cuisine spiced up with the best of Mexican ingredients. French chef Jacques Chretene uses his vast expertise to create such delicacies as tender veal in its juice accented with truffles and asparagus, and fresh Dover sole in white butter sauce studded with bits of lobster. The pastry chef's desserts include mouthwatering soufflés. The wine cellar is nonpareil, and the service impeccable. *Hotel Presidente Inter-Continental México, Campos Elíseos 218, Col. Polanco, tel. 5/327–7700. Reservations essential. Jacket and tie. AE, DC, MC, V. Closed Sun. No lunch Sat.*

$$$–$$$$ LES CÉLÉBRITÉS. In addition to its superb French fare, this
★ elegant hotel restaurant has refreshed the menu with Mediterranean selections. The sunny yellow decor and a profusion of flowers enhance the pleasing light-filled ambience. The restaurant is known for its one-of-a-kind combinations, such as an appetizer of king crab with asparagus cream, sauce of caviar, and passion-fruit vinaigrette; for dessert, there's sinfully rich chocolate mousse cake and light, flaky hazelnut pastry with profiteroles in a chocolate–coriander sauce. The

restaurant is open for breakfast as well. *Nikko México hotel, Campos Elíseos 204, Col. Polanco, tel. 5/280–1111. Reservations essential. Jacket and tie. AE, DC, MC, V. Closed weekends.*

$$$–$$$$ ★ **ESTORIL.** In an exquisitely furnished 1930s town house in fashionable Colonia Polanco, Rosa Martin serves French cuisine with a Mexican flair. *Perejil frito* (fried parsley) is a popular starter, and main dishes offer some unusual combinations: giant prawns in Chablis or curry sauce, and sea bass in fresh coriander sauce. If you have a sweet tooth, try either the delicious tart Tatin—an upside-down apple tart with caramel—or the homemade mint sorbet. *Alejandro Dumas 24, Col. Polanco, tel. 5/280–9828. AE, DC, MC, V. Closed Sun.*

$$$–$$$$ **HACIENDA DE LOS MORALES.** This Mexican institution, set in a former hacienda that dates back to the 16th century, is grandly colonial in style, with dark wood beams, huge terra-cotta expanses, and dramatic torches. The menu combines international and Mexican cuisines with imaginative variations on both. Walnut soup is delicate and unusual. Fish is seemingly unlimited, from sea bass *marinière* (in a white-wine sauce) to a mixed seafood gratin. The charcoal-broiled grain-fed chicken has a distinct flavor. Still, the chef can have his off days, in which case you can head for the tequila bar as consolation. Live mariachi music completes the atmosphere. *Vázquez de Mella 525, Col. Chapultepec Morales, tel. 5/281–4554, 5/281–4703. AE, DC, MC, V. No dinner Sun.*

$$$ **BELLINI.** While its great turntable slowly revolves on the 45th floor of the World Trade Center, executives from surrounding offices pack Bellini at lunch. At night it turns romantic, and the view of the city by lamplight is fantastic. The majority of the dishes here aren't Italian but Mexican and international. The house special is a lobster of your choosing from a tank brought tableside; it's prepared to your taste. Other favorites are filet mignon and homemade pastas served with classic Italian sauces. Finish with a flambéed dessert, such as strawberries jubilee or crêpes suzette. After dinner, work off the extra calories at the disco one floor above the restaurant. *Av. de las Naciones 1, World Trade Center Tower, Col. Napoles,* 20 mins by car south of Zona Rosa, tel. 5/628–8305. Jacket and tie. AE, DC, MC, V.

\$\$–\$\$\$ BELLINGHAUSEN. This is one of the most beloved lunch spots in the Zona Rosa and practically a landmark of good eating for the locals; it's only open until 7 PM. The partially covered hacienda-style courtyard at the back, set off by an ivy-laden wall, is a midday magnet for executives and tourists. A veritable army of waiters scurries back and forth serving such tried-and-true favorites as *sopa de hongos* (mushroom soup) and *filete chemita* (broiled steak with mashed potatoes). The *higaditos de pollo* (chicken livers) with a side order of sautéed spinach is another winning dish. *Londres 95, Zona Rosa,* tel. 5/207–6149. AE, DC, MC, V. No dinner.

\$ LOS ARROCES. The name means "rices," and rice is exactly what you'll get at this trendy spot in Colonia Condesa—50 different rices from around the world in soups, salads, and main dishes—everywhere but desserts. There's *pastel de arroz,* for example, which is white Mexican rice prepared with *rajas* (green pepper strips), *flor de calabaza* (pumpkin flower), corn, and bacon; Maya rice, served with squid, chopped red onion, sour oranges, and beans; and Spanish paella with rice from Valencia. Noteworthy nonrice dishes include chicken with raspberry mole and blue-corn tortilla quesadillas stuffed with cheese, spinach, and chilies. *Michoacán 126,* tel. 5/286–4287. AE, MC, V.

ITALIAN

\$–\$\$ LA LANTERNA. The Petterino family has run this two-story restaurant for more than three decades. The downstairs has the rustic feel of a northern Italian trattoria, with the cramped seating adding to the intimacy. Upstairs is more spacious. All pastas are made on the premises; the Bolognese sauce, in

ONE LAST TRAVEL TIP:

Pack an easy way to reach the world.

MCI WORLDCOM · *WORLDPHONE*

123 456 7891 2345
J.D. SMITH

Wherever you travel, the MCI WorldCom Card℠ is the easiest way to stay in touch. You can use it to call to and from more than 125 countries worldwide. And you can earn bonus miles every time you use your card. So go ahead, travel the world. MCI WorldCom℠ makes it even more rewarding. For additional access codes, visit **www.wcom.com/worldphone**.

MCI WORLDCOM.

EASY TO CALL WORLDWIDE

1. Just dial the WorldPhone® access number of the country you're calling from.

2. Dial or give the operator your MCI WorldCom Card number.

3. Dial or give the number you're calling.

Belgium ◆	0800-10012
Czech Republic ◆	00-42-000112
Denmark ◆	8001-0022
France ◆	0-800-99-0019
Germany ◆	0800-888-8000
Hungary ◆	06▼-800-01411
Ireland	1-800-55-1001
Italy ◆	172-1022
Mexico	01-800-021-8000
Netherlands ◆	0800-022-91-22
Spain	900-99-0014
Switzerland ◆	0800-89-0222
United Kingdom	0800-89-0222
United States	1-800-888-8000

◆ Public phones may require deposit of coin or phone card for dial tone. ▼ Wait for second dial tone.

EARN FREQUENT FLIER MILES

Limit of one bonus program per customer. All airline program rules and conditions apply. © 2000 WorldCom, Inc. All Rights Reserved. The names, logos, and taglines identifying WorldCom's products and services are proprietary marks of WorldCom, Inc. or its subsidiaries. All third party marks are the proprietary marks of their respective owners.

Bureau de change

Cambio

外国為替

In this city, you can find money on almost any street.

NO-FEE FOREIGN EXCHANGE

The Chase Manhattan Bank has over 80 convenient
locations near New York City destinations such as:

        Times Square
        Rockefeller Center
        Empire State Building
        2 World Trade Center
        United Nations Plaza

Exchange any of 75 foreign currencies

 CHASE

THE RIGHT RELATIONSHIP IS EVERYTHING.®

©2000 The Chase Manhattan Corporation. All rights reserved. The Chase Manhattan Bank. Member FDIC.

particular, is a favorite. Raw artichoke salad, *conejo al Salmi* (rabbit in a wine sauce) and *filete al burro nero* (steak in black butter). Seasonal presentations include fungi in a variety of dishes plus homegrown arugula for salads and carpaccio. *Paseo de la Reforma 458, Col. Juárez, tel. 5/207–9969. Reservations not accepted. MC, V. Closed Sun. and Dec. 25–Jan. 1.*

JAPANESE

$$$ SUNTORY. This main branch of the Suntory restaurants in Mexico transports you to Japan by way of a Zen garden at the entryway and a dense green garden that follows. In this enchanted world you are not absolved of the difficulty of choice. Will it be the teppanyaki room to watch your fresh meat or fish prepared with a variety of vegetables, or perhaps the sushi bar— or maybe you'll end up in the shabu-shabu room, with its wafer-thin sashimi and a copper pot of steaming vegetable broth in which elegant slices of beef are cooked? Prices are high, but the ingredients are of the best quality. *Torres Adalid 14, Col. del Valle, tel. 5/536–9432. Second branch: Montes Urales 535, Lomas Chapultepec, tel. 5/202–4711. Reservations essential. AE, DC, MC, V. No dinner Sun.*

MEXICAN

$$$ CICERO CENTENARIO. This thoroughly Mexican restaurant
★ occupies a restored 17th-century mansion in the heart of the historic downtown. Elegant colonial antiques are strikingly posed against folk art and pastel walls, and the bar has an outstanding collection of tin ex-votos and other religious memorabilia. The enticing menu includes excellent versions of authentic colonial dishes such as *pollo en pipián verde* (chicken in green-pumpkin-seed sauce). Try the *chicharrón* (crispy pork rind) and guacamole appetizer, but be sure to leave room for dessert, such as rose-petal ice cream. An ebullient street-level cantina has afternoon serenades by a folk trio. *República de Cuba 79, tel. 5/*

512–1510. *Reservations essential. AE, DC, MC, V. No dinner Sun.*

$$$ **SAN ANGEL INN.** In the south of the city, this magnificent old
★ hacienda and ex-convent, with elegant grounds and
immaculately tended gardens, is both a joy to the eye and an
inspiration to the palate. Dark mahogany furniture, crisp white
table linens, and beautiful blue-and-white Talavera place
settings strike a note of restrained opulence. Many dishes are to
be recommended, especially the classic *huitlacoche* (corn
fungus) served in crepes, as well as *sopa de tortilla* (tortilla soup).
The *puntas de filete* (sirloin tips) are liberally laced with chilies,
and the *huachinango* (red snapper) is offered in a variety of ways.
Desserts—from light and crunchy meringues to pastries
bulging with cream—can be rich to the point of surfeit. *Calle
Diego Rivera 50, at Altavista, Col. San Angel, tel. 5/616–0537, 5/616–
2222, 5/616–1402. Jacket required. AE, DC, MC, V.*

$$–$$$ **EL ARROYO.** This dining complex, complete with its own
bullring, is an attraction in itself. At the south end of town near
the beginning of the highway to Cuernavaca, it was founded
more than 50 years ago by the Arroyo family and is now run by
jovial Jesús ("Chucho") Arroyo. His loyal following includes
celebrities, dignitaries, and bullfighters, along with local
families, groups, and tourists; more than 2,600 people can dine
simultaneously in a labyrinth of 11 picturesque dining areas.
Typical Mexican specialties—chicken mole, a dozen types of
tacos, and much more—are prepared in open kitchens. There's
mariachi music and the full gamut of Mexican drinks, including
pulque, a classic alcoholic Aztec beverage made from a plant
related to the cactus. The small bullring is the forum for
novilleros, or young bullfighters just beginning their careers,
during the season (about April through October). Breakfast
starts at 8 AM, and lunch is served until 8 PM. *Av. Insurgentes Sur
4003, Col. Tlalpán, a 30–40-min drive south of Zona Rosa, tel. 5/573–
4344. AE, DC, MC, V. No dinner.*

$$–$$$ FONDA EL REFUGIO. Since it opened in 1954, this Zona Rosa restaurant in a converted two-story town house has served the best dishes from each major region of the country. Atmosphere is casual but elegant in the intimate colonial-decor dining rooms (the one downstairs is the prettiest). Along with a varied regular menu, there's a daily selection of appetizers and entrées; you might find a mole made with pumpkin seeds or *albóndigas en chile chipotle* (meatballs in chipotle sauce). Try the refreshing *aguas* (fresh-fruit and seed juices) with your meal and the *café de olla* (clove-flavored coffee sweetened with brown sugar) after dessert. *Liverpool 166, Zona Rosa, tel. 5/207–2732, 5/ 525–8128. AE, DC, MC, V. No dinner Sun.*

$$–$$$ ISADORA. Some of Mexico City's most inventive cooking takes place in this converted private house in Polanco. The three smallish dining rooms have a 1920s feel and are uncharacteristically ascetic—pale walls dabbed with minimal modern-artistic flourishes. The management sponsors cooking festivals, and every three months the kitchen produces dishes from a different country. The basic menu changes six times a year, and over that same period it will include three Mexican food fests. The set menu features duck pâté and excellent seafood pasta, with juicy prawns, shellfish, and squid. Ice creams, meringues, and chocolate cake benefit from the chef's delicate mint sauce. *Moliere 50, Col. Polanco, tel. 5/280–1586. Jacket and tie. AE, DC, MC, V. Closed Sun.*

$$–$$$ EL TAJÍN. Named after El Tajín Pyramid in Veracruz, this eatery serves the innovative Mexican cooking that has taken the metropolis by storm. El Tajín adds zest and style to many well-known dishes. Dazzling main dishes include soft-shell crab accented by sesame seeds and a tad of chipotle. This lovely restaurant is hidden behind the functional facade of the Veracruz Cultural Center in Colonia Coyoacán. Ancient Huastecan faces grinning from a splashing fountain add a bit of levity to the dining experience. *Miguel Angel de Quevedo 687, Col. Coyoacán, tel.*

5/659–4447, 5/659–5759. AE, MC, V. No dinner.

$$ LOS ALMENDROS. If you can't make it to the Yucatán, try the peninsula's unusual and lively food. If the spacious, cool white interior and bubbling fountain don't transport you, then the habañero chilies, red onions, and other native Yucatecan ingredients will. Traditional dishes, such as a refreshing lime soup or *frijol con puerco* (tender pork pieces with black beans), share the menu with impossible-to-pronounce Maya cuisine. Especially worth trying is the *pescado tikinxic*—white fish in a mild red marinade of achiote seed and juice of bitter orange. This is a good place to sample a wide array of fine tequila, served with sliced jicama and a tangy tomato-juice chaser called sangrita. *Campos Elíseos 164, Col. Polanco, tel. 5/531–6646. Reservations essential.* AE, D, DC, MC, V.

$$ FONDA DEL RECUERDO. A popular family restaurant, the *fonda*
★ (modest restaurant) also has a solid reputation among tourists and anyone celebrating anything. Every day 2–10, five lively marimba groups from Veracruz provide festive music. The place made its name with its fish and seafood platters from the gulf state of Veracruz, and the house special is huachinango *à la Veracruzano* (a whole red snapper in a succulent, mildly spiced sauce of tomato, chopped onion, and olives). Sharing its fame is the *torito*, a potent drink made from tequila and exotic tropical fruit juices. Meat from the kitchen's own *parillas* (grills) is always first-rate. Portions are huge, but if you have room for dessert, try *crepas de cajeta al tequila* (milk-caramel crepes lightly sauced with tequila). *Bahía de las Palmas 39, Col. Anzures, tel. 5/260–7339, 5/260–1292. Reservations essential.* AE, DC, MC, V.

$$ LOS GIRASOLES. Two prominent Mexico City society columnists own this downtown spot. Los Girasoles (which means sunflowers) is on a lovely old square in a restored three-story colonial home and serves nueva Mexicana cuisine—light, tasty, and innovative. Traditional Mexican bean soup is dressed up with noodles and a pinch of chilies. Meat, fish, and seafood dishes are blended with exotic herbs and spices. There are also pre-Hispanic delicacies such as *escamoles* (ant roe), *gusanos de maguey* (chilied worms), and *chapulines* (crispy fried grasshoppers). The desserts pay homage to local produce with such creations as *guanábana* (soursop) and *zapote* (a tropical fruit native to Mexico) mousses. One of the nicest places for dining is the covered street-level terrace. *Plaza Manuel Tolsa on Xicoténcatl 1, tel. 5/510–0630, 5/510–3281. AE, MC, V. No dinner Sun.*

$$ LOS IRABIEN. This beautiful dining area filled with plants and the owner's impressive art collection is a worthwhile stop for foodies and culture vultures. Chef Arturo Fuentes turns out nueva Mexicana and traditional Mexican dishes. His *ensalada Irabien* triumphs as a mixture of smoked salmon, abalone, prawn, quail eggs, and watercress. One outstanding entrée is nopal cactus stuffed with fish fillet. You'll also find less exotic dishes. Los Irabien is one of the city's breakfast spots par excellence—tempting you with *huevos de codorniz huitzilopochtli*—quail eggs with tortilla in a pumpkin-blossom sauce. *Av. de la Paz 45, Col. San Angel, tel. 5/616–0014. Jacket and tie. AE, DC, MC, V. No dinner Sun.*

$$ T CLA. Since its 1998 opening, this see-and-be-seen newcomer ★ has been a welcome addition to Mexico City's growing nueva Mexicana scene. Named after an old-fashioned typesetting key, the restaurant's Polanco location and a newsprint collage set a hip tone. The artsy Roma locale has copped a bit of an attitude toward those who don't reserve, but the food is worth a little cheekiness. The appetizers are especially intriguing, including squash flowers stuffed with goat cheese in a chipotle sauce and a spicy crab-stuffed chile relleno. The house special beef dish, *filete T Cla*, shows a flair for sauces, in this case combining Roquefort with huitlacoche. Best of all, the prices are still unpretentious. *Moliere 56, Col. Polanco, tel. 5/282–0010; Durango 186A, Col. Roma, tel. 5/525–4920. AE, MC, V. No dinner Sun.*

$ BAJÍO. This cheerful neighborhood bistro is a find when it comes to good eating. Decorated in bright colors, Bajío attracts Mexican families and is run by vivacious Carmen "Titita" Ramírez—a chef and culinary expert who has been featured in, among others, *Saveur* magazine. The restaurant specializes in classic down-home Veracruz cooking. The 30-ingredient mole, a Bajío signature dish, is to die for; also excellent are *empanadas de platano rellenos de frijol* (tortilla turnovers filled with bananas and beans) and *carnitas* (roast pork). You may have to go a little off the beaten track to get here, but it's worth it. *Cuitláhuac 2709, Col. Azcapotzalco, about a 20-min ride north of Zona Rosa, tel. 5/341–9889. AE, MC, V. No dinner.*

$ CAFÉ DE TACUBA. An essential breakfast, lunch, dinner, or snack stop downtown, this Mexican classic has been charming all comers since it opened in 1912 in a section of an old convent. At the entrance to the atmospheric main dining room are huge 18th-century oil paintings depicting the invention of *mole poblano*, a complex sauce with a variety of chilies and chocolate that was created by the nuns in the Santa Rosa Convent of Puebla. Along with mole poblano, look for delicious tamales made fresh every morning. There are also pastries galore. A student group dressed in medieval capes and hats serenades Thursday–Sunday 3:30–11:30; mariachis play during lunch the other days. *Tacuba 28, Col. Centro, tel. 5/518–4950. Reservations not accepted. AE, MC, V.*

$ CASA DE LA SIRENA. Dining is sublime here at the foot of the Templo Major ruins, which supplied some of the building blocks for this 16th-century mansion. A wandering Spanish monk named the home after a mermaid (*sirena*) carved into the facade of a nearby building. The atmospheric second-floor dining terrace is within sight and sound of numerous Indian dances honoring the spirits of the crumbling Aztec temples below. Lunch caters to the vast number of government workers in the area. At night, it's utterly romantic dining under the stars. The cuisine is nouvelle with such specialties as Cornish hen in mango mole sauce and a plethora of other innovative meat and fish dishes. If you've never tried it, order a smooth tequila liqueur as an after-dinner digestive. *Guatemala 32, Zócalo, tel. 5/704–3225, fax 5/704–3465. AE, MC, V. Closed Sun.*

$ **LAS CAZUELAS.** ★ Traditional Mexican cooking at its best is the word at one of the most famous of the capital's fondas. The large dining area is brightened by hand-painted chairs from Michoacán and green-and-white table linens. Ideal Mexican appetizers to share are *carnitas rancheras* (pork morsels in red sauce). The tortilla soup, with its dash of *pasilla* chili and bits of cheese, makes another excellent starter. Main courses center on various moles or the piquant sesame-flavored pipián sauce with pork or chicken. Finish with a café de olla and a domestic brandy. *San Antonio 143, at Illinois, Col. Napoles, tel. 5/563–4118. Reservations not accepted. AE, MC, V. Closed Sun. No dinner.*

$ **FONDA CHON.** This unpretentious family-style restaurant, deep in a downtown working-class neighborhood, is famed for its pre-Hispanic Mexican dishes. A knowledge of zoology, Spanish, and Nahuatl helps in making sense of a menu that takes in a gamut of ingredients—no processed foods among them—from throughout the republic. *Escamoles de hormiga* (red-ant roe), 97% protein, is known as the "caviar of Mexico" for its costliness, but you may have to acquire a taste for it. Among the exotic entrées are armadillo in mango sauce and crackling crisp fried grasshoppers with guacamole. More-traditional specialties include fried or chilied baby kid and barbecued ribs in a red chili sauce. The zapote flan is worth a try. *Regina 160, near La Merced market, Col. Centro, tel. 5/542–0873. Reservations not accepted. MC, V. Closed Sun. No dinner.*

$ **HOSTERIA DE SANTO DOMINGO.** This genteel institution near downtown's Plaza Santo Domingo has been serving *authentico* colonial dishes for more than a century in an atmospheric late-

19th-century town house. Feast on tried-and-true favorites such as stuffed cactus paddles, thousand-flower soup, pot roast, and a stunning array of quesadillas. Among what may be the best homemade Mexican desserts in town are the comforting flan and *arroz con leche* (rice pudding). The place is open for breakfast and is always full at lunch. Get there early to avoid standing in line. *Belisario Dominguez 72, Col. Centro, tel. 5/510–1434, 5/526–5276. AE, MC, V. No dinner Sun.*

SPANISH

$$–$$$ EL PARADOR DE MANOLO. A two-story period house was remodeled into this Spanish restaurant in fashionable Polanco. The Bar Porrón on the ground floor serves Spanish tapas, including an excellent prawn mix in a spicy sauce; after 9, the bar has live music and flamenco. In the brasserie-style dining room upstairs, choose from a Spanish menu or from the list of the chef's recommendations. Specially cured Serrano ham is possibly the best in the city; *calamares fritos* (fried squid) and *crepas de flor de calabaza al gratin* (pumpkin-flower crepes) are other fine starters. Fish dishes make the most appealing main courses, although the chateaubriand Parador for two (in a black corn-fungus sauce) is truly original. Desserts are less notable. Wines are on display downstairs, as are the fresh fish of the day. *Presidente Masarik 433, Col. Polanco, tel. 5/281–2357, 5/281–5762. AE, MC, V. No dinner Sun.*

$$ TEZKA. This Zona Rosa restaurant is Mexico's first and only with nueva cocina Basque, created by famous Basque chef Arzac, who transposed many of his best dishes to Mexico from his restaurant in San Sebastían, Spain. It's always packed with a Spanish clientele. Feast on baked fish in parsley sauce and sweet garlic cream, or pheasant prepared with dates, pine nuts, and apple puree. Arzac disdains appetizers, which he believes ruin appreciation of entrées, so you won't find any starters here. There *are* tempting and original desserts, such as cheese tart with blueberries. There's a decent list of Spanish wines such as Cune, Vina Ardanza, and Reserva 904. *Royal Hotel, Amberes 78, at Liverpool, tel. 5/228–9918. AE, DC, MC, V. Closed Sun. No dinner Sat.*

$–$$ MESON EL CID. This *meson* (tavern) exudes an atmosphere of Old Spain. During the week, classic dishes such as paella, spring lamb, suckling baby pig, and Cornish hens with truffles keep customers happy, but on Saturday night this place really comes into its own with a medieval banquet. The fun unfolds with a procession of costumed waiters carrying huge trays of steaming hot viands. A caged cat—the grandson of the first feline to play this role, the waiters will tell you—heads the parade as in olden days, when a king's food was tested for poisoning by letting a cat nose around in it first (cats being keen enough not to touch the stuff if it had been tampered with). Entertainment is provided by a student singing group dressed in medieval Spanish capes and hats. *Humboldt 61, Col. Centro, tel. 5/521–1940, 5/521–8881, 5/512–7629. AE, MC, V. No dinner Sun.*

VEGETARIAN

$ LAS FUENTES. About three blocks north of the U.S. Embassy on Calle Río Tiber, Las Fuentes is run by Philipe Culbert, a lifelong vegetarian who ascribes to the time-honored dietary dictates of ancient Persia in balancing his menu. A sample meal might be tacos stuffed with carrots and potatoes accompanied by apple salad and followed by whole-grain cookies made with honey. Don't be put off by the sterile Formica tables. The office and embassy workers who pack the place at lunchtime come for the food rather than the ambience. *Río Panuco 27, at Calle Río Tiber, Col. Cuauhtémoc, tel. 5/525–0843. MC, V.*

$ EL JUG. To duck the madding crowd, head for this small, tidy retreat near the Zona Rosa. You'll enjoy delicious vegetarian fare to the accompaniment of New Age music. Heaping salads, homemade soups, and entrées such as *chiles rellenos* (stuffed green peppers) come with whole-grain bread. You can choose the filling daily *comida corrida* (fixed-price menu) or order à la carte. After lunch, you might want to browse through the store on the premises and absorb the vibes of crystals, incense holders, aromatherapy pillows, and the like. *Puebla 326-A (entrance on Calle Cozumel), Col. Roma, tel. 5/553–3872. Reservations not accepted. No credit cards. Closed Sun. No dinner.*

Budget Bites

You can dine very reasonably in Mexico City, but only if you're not scared by the myth that eating at mom-and-pop operations or at street stands will send you running for the bathroom. The food at these places is usually cooked to order, so you can tell if it has been sitting out for too long or hasn't been cooked well enough. If there's a crowd of locals at a certain place, you can bet that the food is good, fresh, and well prepared. A few healthful goodies to look for at street stands citywide include alegrías (large cookies made with amaranth—a whitish grain—and honey), empanadas, and fresh-roasted chestnuts.

That Mexican institution, comida corrida (prepared lunch special), usually beans and rice with a meat entreé, plus coffee and sometimes soup or salad, is a reliable bargain—typically priced at less than $4. Try the restaurants along Isabel la Católica downtown: They usually post their daily comida corrida conspicuously. If you don't mind standing, puestecitos (food stands) almost always surround metro stations. Such places sell everything from tacos de cabeza (made with head meat) to tamarindo (tamarind) candy.

Taco stands as well as stalls that sell fruits and vegetables flourish in the city's markets (just be sure to peel and/or thoroughly wash all produce before consuming it). Or if you have a sudden, uncontrollable hankering for a hamburger there's always the Sanborns or Vips chains, with their hybrid American-Mexican menus.

In This Chapter

Updated by Paige Bierma

shopping

THE FINEST, MOST CONCENTRATED SHOPPING area is the Zona Rosa, a 29-square-block area bounded by Paseo de la Reforma on the north, Niza on the east, Avenida Chapultepec on the south, and Varsovia on the west. It's chock-full of boutiques, jewelry stores, leather-goods shops, antiques stores, and art galleries, as well as dozens of great restaurants and coffee shops. Day or night, the Zona Rosa is always lively.

Polanco, a choice residential neighborhood along the northeast perimeter of Bosque de Chapultepec, has blossomed into a more upscale shopping area with exclusive stores and boutiques. Many are in such malls as the huge ultramodern **Plaza Polanco** (Jaime Balmes 11), the new upscale **Plaza Moliere** (Moliere between Calles Horacio and Homero), and the **Plaza Masarik** (Presidente Masarik and Anatole France).

There are hundreds of shops with more-modest trappings and better prices spread along the length of Avenida Insurgentes, as well as along Avenida Juárez and in the old downtown area.

DEPARTMENT STORES, MALLS, AND SHOPPING ARCADES

The major department-store chains are **Liverpool** (Av. Insurgentes Sur 1310; Mariano Escobedo 425; and in the Plaza Satélite and Perisur shopping centers), **Suburbia** (Horacio 203; Sonora 180; Av. Insurgentes Sur 1235; and in the Plaza Satélite and Perisur shopping centers), and **El Palacio de Hierro** (Calles Durango and Salamanca, Col. Condesa; and in the Plaza

Moliere in Col. Polanco), which is noted for items by well-known designers at prices now on par with those found in the United States. **Santa Fe** mall is the largest in Latin America, with 285 stores, a movie theater, and several restaurants. It's in the elegant Santa Fe district, which in recent years has become the favored office real-estate property in the city. To get here, take the Periférico Expressway south to the exit marked CENTRO SANTA FE. The posh and pricey **Perisur** shopping mall is on the southern edge of the city, near where the Periférico Expressway meets Avenida Insurgentes. Department stores are generally open Monday, Tuesday, Thursday, and Friday 10–7, and Wednesday and Saturday 10–8.

Sanborns is a chain of mini-department stores with some 65 branches in Mexico City. The most convenient are at Madero 4 (its original store in the House of Tiles, downtown); several along Paseo de la Reforma (including one at the Angel monument and another four blocks west of the Diana Fountain); and in the Zona Rosa (one at the corner of Niza and Hamburgo and another at Londres 130 in the Hotel Calinda Geneve). They carry quality ceramics and crafts (and can ship anywhere), and most have restaurants or coffee shops, a pharmacy, ATMs, and periodical and book departments with English-language publications.

Plaza la Rosa, a modern shopping arcade (between Amberes and Génova, Zona Rosa), has 72 prestigious shops and boutiques, including Aldo Conti and Diesel. It spans the depth of the block between Londres and Hamburgo, with entrances on both streets.

Bazar del Centro (at Isabel la Católica 30, just below Calle Madero, downtown) is a restored, late-17th-century noble mansion built around a garden courtyard that houses several chic boutiques and prestigious jewelers such as Aplijsa (tel. 5/ 521–1923), known for its fine gold, silver, pearls, and gemstones, and Ginza (tel. 5/518–6453), which has Japanese pearls, including the prized cultured variety. Other shops sell Taxco silver, Tonalá stoneware, and Mexican tequilas and liqueurs. This complex is elegant and also has a congenial bar.

Portales de los Mercaderes (Merchants' Arcade; extending the length of the west side of the Zócalo between Calles Madero and 16 de Septiembre) has attracted merchants since 1524. It is lined with jewelry shops selling gold (often by the gram) and authentic Taxco silver at prices lower than those in Taxco itself, where the overhead is higher. In the middle of the Portales de los Mercaderes is **Tardán** (Plaza de la Constitución 7, tel. 5/512–2459), an unusual shop specializing in fashionable men's hats of every shape and style.

MARKETS

A "must"—even for browsers—is a visit to the **Bazar Sábado** (Saturday Bazaar) at Plaza San Jacinto in the southern San Angel district. It's been selling unique handicrafts at excellent prices for more than three decades. Outside, vendors sell embroidered clothing, leather goods, wooden masks, beads, *amates* (bark paintings), and trinkets. Inside the bazaar building, a renovated two-story colonial mansion, are the better-quality—and higher-priced—goods, including *alebrijes* (painted wooden animals from Oaxaca), glassware, pottery, jewelry, and papier-mâché flowers. There is an indoor restaurant as well. Market and restaurant are open 10–7.

Sunday 10–4, more than 100 artists exhibit and sell their painting and sculpture at the **Jardín del Arte** (Garden of Art) in Parque Sullivan, just northeast of the Reforma–Insurgentes intersection. Along the west side of the park, a colorful weekend mercado with scores of food stands is also worth a visit.

The **Mercado Insurgentes** (also called Mercado Zona Rosa) is an entire block deep, with entrances on both Londres and Liverpool (between Florencia and Amberes). This is a typical neighborhood public market with one big difference: most of the stalls (222 of them) sell crafts. You can find all kinds of handmade items—including serapes and ponchos, baskets, pottery, silver, pewter, fossils, and onyx, as well as regional Mexican dresses and costumes.

The Zona Rosa's pink neocolonial Plaza del Angel (Londres 161) has a **Centro de Antigüedades** (antiques center) with several fine shops. On Saturday, together with other vendors, the dealers set up a flea market in the arcades and patios. On Sunday, bibliophiles join the antiques vendors to sell, peruse, and buy collectors' books and periodicals.

The Zócalo and Alameda Park areas have interesting markets for browsing and buying handicrafts and curios; polite bargaining is customary. The biggest is the **Centro Artesanal Buenavista** (Aldama 187, by the Buenavista train station, about 1½ km [1 mi] northwest of downtown). **La Lagunilla** market (Libertad, between República de Chile and Calle Allende) attracts antiques hunters who know how to determine authenticity, as well as coin collectors. The best day is Sunday, when flea-market stands are set up outside. This market is known affectionately as the Thieves' Market: local lore says you can buy back on Sunday what was stolen from your home Saturday. Within the colonial walls of **La Ciudadela** market (Balderas and Ayuntamiento, about 4 blocks south of Av. Juárez), more than 300 artisans' stalls display a variety of good handicrafts from all over the country, at better prices than you can find at the rest of the markets.

SPECIALTY SHOPS
Antiques

Antigüedades Coloniart (Estocolmo 37, Zona Rosa, tel. 5/514–4799) has good-quality antique paintings, furniture, and sculpture. The store is open weekdays noon–3 and 4–7, Saturday 10–2. **Antigüedades Imperio** (Hamburgo 149, Zona

Rosa, tel. 5/525–5798) specializes in 19th-century European furniture, paintings, glass, and vases. It's open weekdays 11:30–2 and 3:30–7, Saturday 11:30–3.

Art

The **Juan Martín Gallery** (Dickens 33-B, Col. Polanco, tel. 5/280–0277) is an avant-garde studio. The store and gallery of the renowned **Sergio Bustamante** (Nikko México hotel, Campos Elíseos 204, Col. Polanco, tel. 5/282–2638; Amberes 13, Zona Rosa, tel. 5/525–9059; Camino Real hotel, Mariano Escobedo 700, Col. Polanco, tel. 5/254–7372) displays and sells the artist's wild sculpture, jewelry, and interior-design pieces. The **Oscar Roman Gallery** (Julio Verne 14, Col. Polanco, tel. 5/280–0436) is packed with work by good Mexican painters with a contemporary edge. The **Nina Menocal de Rocha Gallery** (Zacatecas 93, Col. Roma, tel. 5/564–7209) specializes in up-and-coming Cuban painters. **Misrachi** (Presidente Masarik 523, Col. Polanco, tel. 5/250–4105), a veteran among galleries, promotes well-known Mexican and international artists.

Candy

Celaya (5 de Mayo 39, tel. 5/521–1787), in the downtown historic section, is a decades-old haven for those with a sweet tooth. It specializes in candied pineapple, papaya, guava, and other exotic fruit; almond-paste; candied walnut rolls; and *cajeta,* a typical Mexican dessert of thick caramelized milk.

Clothing

The Spanish designer store **Zara** (Londres 102, Zona Rosa, tel. 5/525–1516; Presidente Masarik 332, at Tennyson, Col. Polanco, tel. 5/280–1529; Plaza Moliere, Col. Polanco, tel. 5/280–7572) has sleek women's fashions. **Guess** (Presidente Masarik 326, Col. Polanco, tel. 5/282–0133) sells chic denim sportswear.

Designer Items

Cartier (Amberes 9, Zona Rosa, tel. 5/207–6109; Presidente Masarik 438, Col. Polanco, tel. 5/281–5528) sells genuine designer jewelry and clothes, under the auspices of the French Cartier. **Gucci** (Hamburgo 136, Zona Rosa, tel. 5/207–9997) has no connection with the European store of the same name; nevertheless, it has a fine selection of shoes, gloves, and handbags.

Jewelry

The owner of **Los Castillo** (Amberes 41, Zona Rosa, tel. 5/511–8396) developed a unique method of melding silver, copper, and brass, and is considered by many to be Taxco's top silversmith. His daughter Emilia Castillo displays fine ceramic dishes with tiny inlaid silver figures, such as fish and birds. Taxco silver of exceptional style is sold at **Arte en Plata** (Londres 162-A, Zona Rosa, tel. 5/511–1422), with many designs inspired by pre-Columbian art. **Pelletier** (Torcuato Caso 237, Col. Polanco, tel. 5/250–8600) sells fine jewelry and watches. **Tane** (Amberes 70, Zona Rosa, tel. 5/511–9429; Presidente Masarik 430, Col. Polanco, tel. 5/281–4775; Santa Catarina 207, Col. San Angel, tel. 5/616–0165; and other locations) is a treasure trove of perhaps the best silver work in Mexico—jewelry, flatware, candelabra, museum-quality reproductions of archaeological finds, and bold new designs by young Mexican silversmiths.

Leather

For leather goods you have a couple of choices in Mexico City. **Aries** (Florencia 14, Zona Rosa, tel. 5/533–2509) is Mexico's finest purveyor of leather goods, with a superb selection of bags and accessories for men and women; prices are high. **Gaitán** (Calle Sarasete 95-B, at Tetracini, Col. Peralvillo downtown, tel. 5/759–3393) carries an extensive array of leather coats, luggage, golf bags, and saddles. **Las Bolsas de Coyoacán**

(Carrillo Puerto 9, Col. Coyoacán, tel. 5/554–2010) specializes in high-quality leather goods.

Mexican Crafts

Browse for folk art, sculpture, and furniture in the gallery **Artesanos de México** (Londres 117, Zona Rosa, tel. 5/514–7455). Handwoven wool rugs, tapestries, and fabrics with original and unusual designs can be found at **Tamacani** (Av. Insurgentes Sur 1748B, Col. Florida, tel. 5/662–7133). **Arte Popular en Miniatura** (Hamburgo 85, Col. Juárez, tel. 5/525–8145) is a tiny shop filled with tiny things, from dollhouse furniture and lead soldiers to miniature Nativity scenes. **Flamma** (Hamburgo 167, Zona Rosa, tel. 5/511–8499, 5/511–0266) is a town house that sells beautiful handmade candles. **Galerías del Arcángel** (Estocolmo 40, Zona Rosa, tel. 5/511–6303) is an exquisite crafts and furniture shop tucked away in the Zona Rosa. It specializes in carved wood furniture from Patzcuaro, Michoacán (brought to life with brightly painted sunflowers, calla lilies, and suns), as well as wooden angel decorations, pottery, and paintings.

Under the auspices of the National Council for Culture and Arts, **Fonart** (National Fund for Promoting Handicrafts) operates two stores in Mexico City, and others around the country. Prices are fixed (and high), but the diverse, top-quality folk art and hand-crafted furnishings from all over Mexico represent the best artisans. The best location is downtown (Juárez 89, tel. 5/521–0171), just west of Alameda Park. Major sales at near wholesale prices are held at the main store–warehouse (Av. Patriotismo 691, Col. Mixcoac, tel. 5/563–4060) year-round.

Feders (factory: Bufon 25, Col. Nueva Anzures, tel. 5/260–2958; Bazar Sábado booth, Plaza San Jacinto 11, San Angel, tel. no phone) has great handblown glass, Tiffany-style lamps, and wrought iron.

In This Chapter

Updated by Paige Bierma

outdoor activities and sports

WATCHING A GAME OF FÚTBOL, Mexico City's most popular sport, in the second-largest stadium in Latin America is almost as thrilling as a bullfighting match—if you can stomach it—in the world's largest bullring. The really adventurous can take a trip out of the city and up a volcano or down some river rapids.

ADVENTURE SPORTS

A number of adventure-travel agencies have sprouted up to lead both tourists and natives on white-water rafting, rappelling, or biking trips. One of the best is **México Verde Expeditions** (Homero 526, Int. 801, Col. Polanco, tel. 5/255–4400, 5/255–4465), whose guides speak English. Call a week in advance to make reservations and bring a sleeping bag and sunblock. The small **Planeta Expeditions** (Amatlán 51-C, at Montes de Oca, tel. 5/211–9020) is run out of a café in trendy Colonia Condesa. It has journeys to climb the Iztaccíhuatl volcano, as well as rafting and rock climbing.

BULLFIGHTING

The main season is the dry season, around November through March, when celebrated *matadores* appear at **Plaza México** (Calle Agusto Rodín 241, at Holbein, Col. Ciudad de los Deportes, tel. 5/563–3959), the world's largest bullring, which seats 40,000. Tickets, about $2–$25, can be purchased at hotel travel desks or at the bullring's ticket booths weekends 9:30–2 and 3:30–7. The ring is next to the Ciudad de los Deportes sports complex, and the show goes on at 4 Sunday.

GOLF

All golf courses are private in Mexico City, but you can play if you are the guest of a member. If you stay at the Camino Real hotel, you can have the hotel arrange admittance to the **Bella Vista Golf Club** (tel. 5/360–3501), off the Querétaro Highway. Greens fees Tuesday through Friday are $85; weekends, $150.

SOCCER

Fútbol is the sport that Mexicans are most passionate about, which is evident in the size of their soccer stadium, **Estadio Azteca** (Calzada de Tlalpan 3465), the second largest in Latin America. The World Cup Finals were held here in 1970 and 1986. You can buy tickets outside the stadium in the south of the city on the same day of any minor game. For more-important games, buy tickets a week in advance. The Pumas, a popular university-sponsored team, play at **Estadio Olímpica** (Av. Insurgentes Sur at Universidad Nacional Autónoma de México).

TENNIS

Tennis clubs are private in Mexico, so if you want to play, consider staying at a hotel that has courts on site.

WATER SPORTS

The best place for swimming is your hotel pool. If you're desperate to row a boat, however, you can rent one in the lakes of Bosque de Chapultepec, near the Zoológico.

Distance Conversion Chart

Kilometers/Miles

To change kilometers (km) to miles (mi), multiply km by .621.
To change mi to km, multiply mi by 1.61.

km to mi	mi to km
1 = .62	1 = 1.6
2 = 1.2	2 = 3.2
3 = 1.9	3 = 4.8
4 = 2.5	4 = 6.4
5 = 3.1	5 = 8.1
6 = 3.7	6 = 9.7
7 = 4.3	7 = 11.3
8 = 5.0	8 = 12.9

Meters/Feet

To change meters (m) to feet (ft), multiply m by 3.28.
To change ft to m, multiply ft by .305.

m to ft	ft to m
1 = 3.3	1 = .30
2 = 6.6	2 = .61
3 = 9.8	3 = .92
4 = 13.1	4 = 1.2
5 = 16.4	5 = 1.5
6 = 19.7	6 = 1.8
7 = 23.0	7 = 2.1
8 = 26.2	8 = 2.4

In This Chapter

Updated by Paige Bierma

nightlife and the arts

GOOD PLACES TO CHECK for events include the Friday edition of *The News*, a daily English-language newspaper, and *Tiempo Libre*, a weekly magazine listing activities and events in Spanish. All are available at newsstands.

Citywide cultural festivals with free music, dance, and theater performances by local groups take place all year long but especially in July and August. A three-week spring cultural festival with international headliners takes place in the Historic Center between March and April. Check with the Mexico City Tourist Office (☞ Practical Information) for dates and details.

THE ARTS
Dance

The world-renowned **Ballet Folklórico de México,** directed by Amalia Hernández, presents stylized Mexican regional folk dances and is one of the most popular shows in Mexico. Performances Wednesday at 8:30 PM and Sunday at 9:30 AM and 8:30 PM are at the beautiful Palacio de Bellas Artes (Palace of Fine Arts; Av. Juárez at Eje Central Lázaro Cárdenas)—it's a treat to see its Tiffany-glass curtain lowered. Call the Palacio de Bellas Artes box office (tel. 5/512–3633) or Ticketmaster (tel. 5/325–9000) for information on prices and for reservations. Hotels and travel agencies can also secure tickets.

The **National Dance Theater** (tel. 5/280–8771), behind the National Auditorium on Paseo de la Reforma, and the **Miguel**

Covarrubias Hall (National Autonomous University of Mexico [UNAM], Av. Insurgentes Sur 3000, Ciudad Universitaria, tel. 5/622–7051 for university's dance department) frequently sponsor modern-dance performances.

Music

The primary venue for classical music is the **Palacio de Bellas Artes** (Eje Central Lázaro Cárdenas and Av. Juárez, tel. 5/512–3633), which has a main auditorium and the smaller Manuel Ponce concert hall. The National Opera has two seasons at the palace: January–March and August–October. The National Symphony Orchestra stages classical and modern pieces at the palace in the spring and fall.

The top concert hall, often touted as the best in Latin America, is **Ollin Yolitzli** (Periférico Sur 5141, tel. 5/606–7573); it hosts the Mexico City Philharmonic several times a year. The National Autonomous University of Mexico's Philharmonic orchestra performs at **Nezahualcoyotl Hall** (National Autonomous University of Mexico, Av. Insurgentes Sur 3000, Ciudad Universitaria, tel. 5/622–7112).

For pop music stars such as Jamiroquai, Luis Miguel, Kiss, and Juan Gabriel, check newspapers for attractions at the following halls: **Auditorio Nacional** (Paseo de la Reforma 50, across from Nikko México hotel, tel. 5/280–9234, 5/280–9979), **Teatro Metropolitano** (Independencia 90, downtown, tel. 5/510–1035, 5/510–1045), **Palacio de los Deportes** (Av. Río Churubusco and Calle Añil, tel. 5/237–9999 ext. 4264), and **Hard Rock Cafe** (Paseo de la Reforma and Campos Elíseos, Col. Condesa, tel. 5/327–7171).

Theater

You might find some English-language plays by checking listings in The News. However, if you understand Spanish (or are content to watch), you'll be able to enjoy a wider range of theatrical entertainment in Mexico City, including recent Broadway hits. Prices are reasonable compared with those for stage productions of similar caliber in the United States. Although Mexico City has no central theater district, most theaters are within a 15- to 30-minute taxi ride from the major hotels. The top venues include **Hidalgo** (Av. Hidalgo 23, at Eje Central Lázaro Cárdenas, tel. 5/521–5859), **Insurgentes** (Av. Insurgentes Sur 1587, tel. 5/598–6894), **Silvia Pinal** (Yucatán 160, at Coahuila, Col. Roma, tel. 5/264–1172), **Teatros Alameda** (Av. Cuauhtémoc at Av. Chapultepec, tel. 5/514–2300, ext. 221 or 244), and **Virginia Fabregas** (Joaquín Velázquez de León 29, tel. 5/566–4321). Theater tickets are available through **Ticketmaster** (tel. 5/325–9000).

NIGHTLIFE

Night is the key word to understanding the timing of going out in Mexico City. People generally have cocktails at 7 or 8, take in dinner and a show at 10 or 11, head to discos at midnight, then find a spot for a nightcap somewhere around 3 AM. The easiest way to do this if you don't speak Spanish is on a nightlife tour. If you set off on your own you should have no trouble getting around, but for personal safety absolutely avoid taking taxis off the street—take official hotel taxis or call a *sitio* (stationed) taxi (☞ Taxis in Practical Information).

Niza and Florencia streets in the Zona Rosa are practically lined with nightclubs, bars, and discos that are especially lively Friday and Saturday nights. Big hotels have both bars and places to dance or be entertained, and they are frequented by locals. Outside the Zona Rosa, Paseo de la Reforma and Avenida Insurgentes Sur have the greatest concentration of nightspots. Mexico City has something for everyone in the way of night entertainment, but remember that the capital's high altitude makes liquor extremely potent, even jolting. Imported booze is very expensive, so you may want to stick with what the Mexicans order: tequila, rum, and *cerveza* (beer).

Dancing

Dance emporiums in the capital run the gamut from cheek-to-cheek romantic to throbbing strobe lights and ear-splitting music. Most places have a cover charge, but it is rarely more than $10. Some of the clubs require that reservations be made one to two days beforehand for Thursday through Saturday nights, if you want a table.

To really experience the nightlife Mexico has to offer, it's imperative to visit a dance club. **Bar León** (República de Brasil 5, Col. Centro, behind the Catedral Metropolitana in the Zócalo, tel. 5/510–2979) is a traditional salsa bar with great live music and a kitschy feel. **Salón Los Ángeles** (Lerdo 206, Col. Guerrero, tel. 5/597–5181) takes you back in time to the 1930s, with decor straight out of a movie. The grand, open dance floor swings to the rhythms of danzón and salsa. When renowned musicians such as Celia Cruz come to town, this is where they perform. The popular **Salón México** (2do Callejón San Juan de Dios 25, tel. 5/518–0931) is a Colonia Guerrero danzón spot. **Meneo** (Nueva York 315, Col. Napoles, just off Av. Insurgentes Sur, tel. 5/523–9448) is a modern dance hall for live salsa and merengue with two dance floors. One of the capital's best-kept secrets is **Mama Rumba** (Querétaro 230, at Medillín, Col. Roma, tel. 5/564–6920), a 10-minute cab ride from the Zona Rosa. A nondescript Cuban restaurant during the day, it turns on the hot salsa, danzón, cha-cha-cha, and conga beat Thursday, Friday, and Saturday nights, when the top-rate Cuban house band takes the stand. Both Bar León and Mama Rumba are great if you aren't an expert dancer because the tiny dance floors are so packed that no one will notice mistakes.

If Latin music isn't your thing, two of the hippest discos in the city stand next to each other in the center. The **Pervert Lounge**

(Uruguay 70½, Col. Centro, tel. 5/518–0976) and **Colmillo** (Fang; Versailles 52, Col. Juárez, tel. 5/518–0976) are swank, upscale places where the young and beautiful come to see and be seen while shaking their exposed belly buttons on the dance floor. The Colmillo spins techno music downstairs and has an exclusive jazz bar upstairs.

Bars

Nice bars to sit and have a few drinks in are hard to come by in Mexico City. Often they are either too noisy or too seedy. Bars are usually open Tuesday–Saturday 8–3 and generally don't charge a cover. However, **La Nueva Ópera** (5 de Mayo 10, at Filomeno Mata, downtown, tel. 5/512–8959) is one of the city's finest cantinas, and it's brought in top personalities since it opened in 1870. The bar provides a relaxing atmosphere, Mexican appetizers and entrées, and an expansive drink list. Don't forget to have your waiter point out the bullet hole allegedly left in the ceiling by Mexican revolutionary hero Pancho Villa. **Bar Milán** (Milán 18, at General Prim, Col. Juárez, tel. 5/592–0031) is a very casual, unpretentious local favorite. Upon entering you need to change pesos into *milagros* (miracles), which are notes necessary to buy drinks throughout the night. The catch is to remember to change them back for pesos before last call. The music tends to be the latest alternative grooves, Latin rock, and '80s singers such as Diana Ross. Make sure to check out the amazing cactus sculpture covering the wall behind the main bar. **Bar Mata** (Filomeno Mata 11, at 5 de Mayo, tel. 5/518–0237) is on the fourth and fifth floors of a colonial building near Palacio de Bellas Artes in the centro. The atmosphere is conducive to dancing and mingling, especially in the rooftop (fifth floor) bar, which has great views of the night-lit city and is a place to escape from the cigarette smoke.

Dinner Shows

The liveliest shows are in clubs downtown and in the Zona Rosa. The **Feria de México** (Paseo de la Reforma 28, across from Meliá

México Reforma hotel, tel. 5/535–1065) is the newest venue for enjoying traditional Mexican music and dance over dinner. Show times at this rustic dinner club are 4 and 10:30 daily, with an additional 6:30 show Thursday through Saturday. The show is free, but you pay for your meal (varied Mexican–American fare) à la carte. At **Focolare** (Hamburgo 87, at Río Niza, tel. 5/207–8257), you can watch a cock fight, mariachi singers, and traditional folk dancers Thursday through Saturday nights. The show costs $7.50; Mexican dinner and drinks are separate. At the **Hotel de Cortés** (Hidalgo 85, downtown, tel. 5/518–2184) you can take in the strains of marimba and mariachi players as well as watch traditional dancers on the beautiful patio. The show goes on Friday night only and for $20 includes a full meal.

Hotel Bars

The following hotel-lobby bars are all good bets for a sophisticated crowd and more-mellow music, about 7–1 daily: **María Isabel Sheraton** (Paseo de la Reforma 325, Col. Cuauhtémoc, tel. 5/207–3933), **Presidente Inter-Continental México** (Campos Elíseos 218, Col. Polanco, tel. 5/327–7700), **Camino Real** (Mariano Escobedo 700, Col. Nueva Anzures, tel. 5/203–2121), and **Galería Plaza** (Hamburgo 195, Zona Rosa, tel. 5/208–0370).

Mariachi Music

The traditional last stop for nocturnal Mexicans is **Plaza Garibaldi** (east of Eje Central Lázaro Cárdenas, between República de Honduras and República de Perú), where exuberant mariachis gather to unwind after evening performances—by performing even more. There are roving mariachis, as well as *norteño* (country-style) music and white-clad *jarocho* bands (Veracruz-style), peddling songs in the outdoor plaza, where you can also buy beer and shots of tequila. Well-to-do Mexicans park themselves inside one of the cantinas or clubs surrounding the plaza and belt out their favorite songs with the hired musicians.

The better cantinas are Guadalajara de Noche (tel. 5/526–5521) and Tenampa (tel. 5/526–6341). Choose a cantina and order a tequila; the musicians will be around shortly offering to serenade you (a song costs about $5). Mexicans typically buy songs by the dozen, so the bar is rarely without the wailing mariachis for more than 10 minutes. These places stay open Sunday through Thursday until at least 2 AM, and even later Friday and Saturday.

Note: The square was spruced up in the early '90s to rid it of its seedy image, but things can still get a bit raucous late at night. Furthermore, leaving Plaza Garibaldi can be dangerous—be sure to arrange for transportation ahead of time. You may call a travel agency, drive your car and park in the well-lighted ramp below the plaza, or call a safe sitio taxi (☞ Taxis in Practical Information).

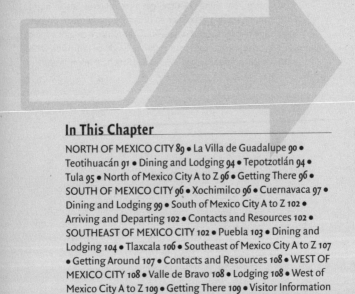

In This Chapter

Updated by Paige Bierma

side trips

ALTHOUGH THE URBAN lifestyle in Mexico City is steeped in American culture, you'll be pleasantly surprised to find that just a short drive or bus ride can place you in a traditional small-town church, in the middle of a gorgeous national park, or on top of breathtaking ancient ruins. Quaint towns give a taste of what life might have been like in Mexico City before its population began exploding with industrial growth in the 1960s and '70s. Just an hour north of the city, the famous Teotihuacán ruins have larger and more historically significant pyramids, as do the former Toltec capital of Tula.

Two nearby state capitals, the medium-size cities of Cuernavaca and Puebla, are windows on the diversity of Mexican life. Cuernavaca's flower power and springlike climate have made this culturally hip city a favorite weekend getaway for *chilangos* (Mexico City residents), as well as a center for Spanish-language schools that draw people from around the world. Puebla, on the other hand, is a conservative city, surrounded by important agricultural valleys and populated with an abundance of churches, chapels, ex-convents, and monasteries.

NORTH OF MEXICO CITY

Hugging the roads to the north of Mexico City are several of the country's most celebrated pre-Columbian and colonial monuments. The Basílica de Guadalupe, a church dedicated to Mexico's patron saint, and the pyramids of Teotihuacán make an easy day tour, as does the combination of the ex-convent (now a magnificent museum of the viceregal period) at Tepotzotlán and the ruins at Tula, also to the north but in a slightly different direction.

There are no tourist offices in the area, but a good English-language guidebook to Teotihuacán is sold at the site.

LA VILLA DE GUADALUPE

"La Villa"—the local moniker of the site of the two basilicas of the Virgin of Guadalupe—is Mexico's holiest shrine. Its importance derives from the miracle that the devout believe transpired here on December 12, 1531, when an Indian named Juan Diego received from the Virgin a cloak permanently imprinted with her image so he could prove to the priests that he had indeed had a holy vision. On that date each year millions of pilgrims arrive, many crawling on their knees for the last few hundred yards, praying for cures and other divine favors. When Pope John Paul II visited Mexico in 1999, he blessed the new statue of Juan Diego located outside the **Antigua Basílica** (Old Basilica). The Antigua Basílica dates from 1536; various additions have been made since then. The altar was executed by sculptor Manuel Tolsá. The basilica now houses a museum of ex-votos (hand-painted tin retablos) and popular religious art, paintings, sculpture, and decorative and applied arts from the 15th to the 18th centuries.

Because the structure of the Antigua Basílica had weakened over the years and the building was no longer large enough or safe enough to accommodate all the worshipers, Pedro Ramírez Vázquez, the architect responsible for Mexico City's splendid National Museum of Anthropology, was commissioned to design a new shrine; it was consecrated in 1976. In this case, alas, the architect's inspiration failed him: the **Nueva Basílica** is a grotesque and most unspiritual mass of steel, wood, resinous fibers, and polyethylene. The famous cloak is enshrined in its own altar and can be viewed from a moving sidewalk that passes below it.

TEOTIHUACÁN

This Mesoamerican Giza is one of the most powerful sites in Mexico; from its size and scale, there's no doubting Teotihuacán's (*teh-oh-tee-wa-can*) monumental place in history. It was likely a small town already by 100 BC; four centuries later it had reached its zenith. At the time of its decline in the 8th century, it was one of the largest cities in the world, with possibly as many as 250,000 people. The sacred metropolis lay in the midst of rich obsidian mines, which provided the means for its rise as a major regional trading power and center for the arts— its influence on Maya pottery stretched as far away as Tikal in present-day Guatemala. The glasslike obsidian is still being fashioned into animal figures, which are sold in market stalls on the site. Just who lived here isn't exactly clear—even the original name of the city is lost. It is believed that water shortages and crises caused by local deforestation contributed to Teotihuacán's downfall. It was set on fire and destroyed by raiders around AD 650. Centuries later, the Aztecs arrived in the Valley of Mexico. Because the memory of the grandeur of this city survived the passage of time, these new settlers named the site Teotihuacán, which meant "place where the gods were born." It was here, the Aztecs believed, that the gods created the universe.

The awesome **Pirámide del Sol** (Pyramid of the Sun), with a base as broad as that of the pyramid of Cheops in Egypt, is off the center of Teotihuacán's main axis. Estimated to have been built between AD 100 and AD 250, it is the site's oldest structure. Its planes and angles were precisely built in relation to the movement of the sun—marking the equinoxes, for example— and the Pleiades constellation. The 242 steps of the 215-ft pyramid face west, the cardinal point where it was believed that

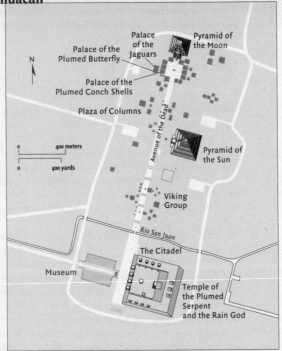

Palace of the Plumed Butterfly

Palace of the Jaguars

Palace of the Plumed Conch Shells

Pyramid of the Moon

Plaza of Columns

N

Avenue of the Dead

0 — 400 meters
0 — 400 yards

Pyramid of the Sun

Viking Group

Río San Juan

The Citadel

Museum

Temple of the Plumed Serpent and the Rain God

the sun was transformed into a jaguar in order to pass nightly through the darkness of death.

The most impressive sight in Teotihuacán is the 4-km- (2½-mi-) long **Calzada de los Muertos** (Avenue of the Dead), the main axis of the ancient city along which six major structures lie. The Aztecs gave the avenue this name because of the stepped platforms lining it, which they mistook for tombs. The graceful 126-ft-high **Pirámide de la Luna** (Pyramid of the Moon) dominates the northern end of the avenue, and the compact, square **Ciudadela** (Citadel) flanks the opposite end. More than 4,000 one-story dwellings constructed of adobe and stone and occupied by artisans, warriors, and tradesmen once surrounded the avenue. On the west side of the spacious plaza facing the Pyramid of the Moon are the **Palacio del Quetzalpápalotl** (Palace of the Plumed Butterfly), **Templo de las Conchas Emplumados** (Temple of Plumed Conch Shells), and **Palacio de los Jaguares** (Palace of Jaguars), which is where the priests resided. The palaces are best known for the spectacular bird and jaguar murals in their winding underground chambers.

The Ciudadela, with its **Templo de Quetzalcóatl y Tlaloc** (Temple of the Plumed Serpent and Rain God), shows off the plastic arts of the time with its brawny toothed serpent heads jutting out of the temple facade. Quetzalcóatl and Tlaloc together represent the fusion of earth and sky.

Climbing one pyramid is probably enough for most people. The Pyramid of the Sun is the taller by 89 ft, and affords a spectacular view of the entire area. Wear comfortable clothes (especially shoes) and bring sunscreen or a visored hat when you visit.

Many of the artifacts uncovered at Teotihuacán are on display at the Museum of Anthropology in Mexico City. The **on-site museum,** opened in 1994 near the Pyramid of the Sun, contains fabulous pieces from the archaeological zone—such as the stone sculpture of Tlaloc, the goggle-eyed god of rain; black and green obsidian arrowheads; and simulated burial sites of exalted personages of the empire, their skeletons arranged as they were when discovered.

Seeing the ruins will take two–four hours, depending on how smitten you are by the place—or when your tour bus leaves. *tel. 595/60052 or 595/60276. $2.50, free Sun. Daily 7–6.*

Many tour buses to the ruins stop briefly in **San Agustín Acolmán** to see the outstanding plateresque (an ornate 16th-century Spanish style) church and ex-convent, now a museum.

The original Augustinian church (1539) is noteworthy for its vaulted roof and pointed towers. The ornate cloister and plateresque facade, set off with candelabralike columns, were added a century later by the monks.

Dining and Lodging

For price categories, *see* Eating Out *and* Where to Stay.

$$ **Villa Arqueológica.** If you'd like to overnight at the pyramids, this Club Med stands across the road from the fenced-off site and has snug rooms and a huge garden and patio restaurant-bar surrounding a pool and tennis court. This is the only hotel that has permission to be in the area. *Villa Arqueológica Teotihuacán, San Juan de Teotihuacán 55800, tel. 595/60909, 5/203–3086 in Mexico City, 800/258–2633. 40 rooms. Restaurant, pool, tennis court. AE, MC, V.*

TEPOTZOTLÁN

The **Jesuit church** and **school of San Francisco Javier** at Tepotzotlán (pronounced teh-po-tzot-lan) rank among the masterpieces of Mexican churrigueresque architecture. The unmitigated Baroque facade of the church (1682) is the first thing to catch the eye, but inside and out, every square inch has been worked over, like an overdressed Christmas tree. Note the gilded, mirrored Chapel of the Virgin of Loreto.

In pre-Hispanic times, the village was an important stop along the salt route—salt was used as money—between Toluca and Texcoco (near Teotihuacán) and had a prestigious school of dance and art. In 1580, four Jesuit priests arrived, learned the native language, and turned the village into a center of evangelization by setting up a school for the young nobles of the conquered nation. The church, of course, was built with Indian slave labor, but as a concession to the slaves, many of the angels decorating the chambers have been painted with dark-skinned indigenous faces. This is probably the only church in Mexico where you will find such paintings. There's also a museum of religious art in the complex. There are two notable restaurants for taking a light snack or lunch after viewing the Jesuit complex. One is the museum's coffee shop and the other is **Casa Mago,** directly across the square from the church. Casa Mago's owners will proudly recount how Elizabeth Taylor dropped by in 1963 to have a beer.

This village is also famous for its traditional Christmas *pastorela*, a charming and humorous morality play that has been taking place for more than 30 years, telling the story of the birth of Jesus Christ. Staged every year December 16–23 in the patio of the church at night, the cast includes a few professionals and loads of extras from the town who portray shepherds, angels, and, of course, the Devil. Tickets are available through Ticketmaster (tel. 5/325–9000 in Mexico City) or the church's offices in Tepotzotlán (tel. 5/876–0243).

TULA

Tula, capital of the Toltecs—whose name for it was Tollán—was founded around AD 1000 and abandoned two centuries later. Quetzalcóatl was born in Tula and became its priest-king. Under his rule, the Toltecs reached the pinnacle of their civilization, with art, science, and philosophy flourishing. According to myth, Quetzalcóatl went into exile in Yucatán but vowed to return—on a date (1519) that unfortunately coincided with the arrival of Hernán Cortés, whom the Aztecs therefore fatefully welcomed. Visible from afar, Tula's 15-ft **warrior statues** (*atlantes*), rather than the ruins themselves, make the show. These basalt figures tower over Pyramid B, their strong geometrics looking vaguely totemic. Crocodiles, jaguars, coyotes, and eagles are also depicted in the carvings and represent the various warrior orders of the Toltecs. $2, *free Sun.* Tues.–Sun. 9:30–4:30.

NORTH OF MEXICO CITY A TO Z
Getting There

To get to **La Villa de Guadalupe** by car, take Paseo de la Reforma Norte until it forks into Calzada de Guadalupe, which leads directly to the shrine. Or take the No. 3 (red) metro line from downtown to the Basílica stop (the station symbol is the virgin's image). Buses run every 20 minutes between 7 AM and 3 PM from the Central de Autobuses del Norte to **Teotihuacán,** and the trip takes about one hour. Tour companies also offer combination visits to the two sights.

To get to **Tepotzlán** from Mexico City, follow Periférico Norte. After 41 km (25 mi), you'll come to the exit for Tepotzotlán. **Tula** is about 8 km (5 mi) north of Tepotzotlán. Buses to Tula/Tepotzotlán leave Mexico City every 20 minutes, also from the Central de Autobuses del Norte.

SOUTH OF MEXICO CITY

Xochimilco (pronounced kso-chee-*meel*-co) is famous for its floating gardens, where you can ride in gondolalike boats and get a fleeting sense of a pre-Hispanic Mexico City. Beyond Xochimilco, in the neighboring state of Morelos, Cuernavaca is a weekend retreat for wealthy chilangos and foreigners.

XOCHIMILCO

When the first nomadic settlers arrived in the Valley of Mexico, they found an enormous lake. As the years went by and their population grew, the land wasn't sufficient to satisfy their agricultural needs. They solved the problem by devising a system of *chinampas* (floating gardens), rectangular structures something like barges, which they filled with reeds, branches, and mud. They planted them with willows, whose roots anchored the floating gardens to the lake bed, making a labyrinth of small islands and canals on which they carried the flowers and produce grown on the chinampas to market.

Today Xochimilco is the only place in Mexico where the gardens still exist. Go on a Saturday, when the *tianguis* (market) is most active, or on a Sunday. (Note that Xochimilco is popular among families on Sunday.) On weekdays the place is practically deserted, so it loses much of its charm. Hire a *trajinera* (flower-painted launch); an arch over each spells out its name in flowers. As you sail through the canals, you'll pass mariachis and women selling tacos from other trajineras.

★ People also flock to Xochimilco for the **Museo Dolores Olmedo Patiño,** which holds the largest private collection of works by flamboyant muralist Diego Rivera. It was put together by Olmedo, his lifelong model, patron, and onetime mistress (which she denies). The lavish display of nearly 140 pieces from his cubist, post-cubist, and mural periods hangs in a magnificent 17th-century hacienda with beautiful gardens. The museum also has works by Rivera's legal wife, Frida Kahlo, and his common-law wife, Angelina Beloff. *Av. México 5843, tel. 5/ 555–1016. $2. Tues.–Sun. 10–6.*

CUERNAVACA

The climate in Cuernavaca, a trifling 85 km (53 mi) from Mexico City, changes dramatically to lush and semitropical as the altitude descends almost 2,500 ft. In fact, it was this balmy springlike temperature that first attracted the rich and famous to what has become a resort: Cortés built the first summer place—read palace—here in the 16th century. There are spectacular restaurants and hotels, in addition to the beautiful Borda Gardens and Diego Rivera murals in the Palacio de Cortés. An overnight stay is recommended.

Cuernavaca is built on a series of small hills whose streets intertwine at a maddening pace. If you're not used to driving in San Francisco, say, it's better to get around by cab, especially on weekends, when the number of cars swells to disproportionate numbers.

Most sights are concentrated around the central **Plaza de Armas,** which is surrounded by crafts shops, sidewalk cafés, and government buildings. The square itself is filled with vendors from neighboring villages. Throughout the week they hawk local arts and crafts; on weekends, one side of the square is taken over by stalls in which you'll find silver and gold jewelry and leather goods from elsewhere in the country. **Jardín Juárez** (Juárez Gardens), a smaller square across the street from Plaza de Armas, puts on free band concerts Thursday evening at 6 under its colonial arcade. Either of these two squares is the perfect place for whiling away a pleasant afternoon after a visit to the tourist sights. After dark, the hip spot is the **Plazuela del Zacate** (Galeana and Fray Bartolomé de Las Casas, 2 blocks from the Plaza de Armas), where sidewalk cafés and bars open every night and young people gather.

The **Palacio de Cortés** (Cortés's palace-cum-fortress) houses the **Museo de Cuauhnáhuac**—Cuauhnáhuac being the native name for Cuernavaca—which focuses on Mexican history before and after the conquest. Diego Rivera painted some of his finest murals on the palace's top floor in 1930–32. Like those of Mexico City's National Palace, they dramatize the history and the horrors of the conquest, colonialism, and the revolution. Former U.S. Ambassador to Mexico Dwight Morrow commissioned Rivera to paint the murals for $30,000. *Juárez and Hidalgo, tel. 73/12–81–71. $1.60, free Sun. Tues.–Sun. 10–5.*

The beautiful, spacious **Jardín Borda** (Borda Gardens) is the most visited sight in Cuernavaca. The jardín was designed in the late 18th century by a member of the Borda family—rich miners of French extraction—for one of his relatives; Maximilian and Carlotta visited the gardens frequently. Here Maximilian had a dalliance with the gardener's wife, La India Bonita, who was immortalized in a portrait by a noted painter of the time. In this century, novelist Malcolm Lowry turned the gardens into a sinister symbol in *Under the Volcano. Av. Morelos 103, at Hidalgo, 3 blocks west of Palacio de Cortés, tel. 73/12–92–37. $1, free Sun. Tues.–Sun. 10–5:30.*

The **Catedral de la Asunción,** an eclectic structure begun in 1529 by Cortés, is noteworthy for the skull and crossbones over its main entrance and its 17th-century Japanese wall paintings. It's also famous for Sunday-morning mariachi masses. Paintings inside the **Palacio Municipal,** diagonally opposite the cathedral, depict pre-Hispanic city life. *Hidalgo and Av. Morelos, opposite Borda Gardens.*

Near Plaza de Armas, the **Robert Brady Museum** is a delightful restored colonial mansion housing a diverse collection of art and artifacts assembled by the late Brady—an artist, antiquarian, and decorator from Fort Dodge, Iowa. You can see ceramics, antique furniture, sculptures, paintings, and tapestries, all beautifully arranged in rooms painted with bright Mexican colors. *Calle Netzahuacóyotl 4, between Hidalgo and Abasolo, tel. 73/18–85–54. $2. Tues.–Sun. 10–6.*

The small ruins of **Xochicalco** ("place of flowers") include a pyramid and ball court. Showing Maya, Toltec, and Zapotec influences, the ancient fortified city reached its peak between AD 700 and 900. A solar-powered museum has six rooms of artifacts, including beautiful sculptures of Xochicalco deities found on site. The museum has a café, bookstore, and gift shop. *23 mi southwest of Cuernavaca (take Hwy. 95D south; look for the sign for the turnoff). tel. No phone. $2, free Sun. Tues.–Sun. 10–5.*

Dining and Lodging

If you've missed getting invited to one of the wealthy weekenders' mansions set in the hills on the edge of town, not to worry: there are a number of remarkable hotels and restaurants with equally remarkable gardens—several of them in restored colonial mansions and even haciendas—where you can get a taste of life behind the high stone walls. Many people come here to do just that, and many Cuernavaca hostelries that began as restaurants added on rooms to satisfy clients who felt too relaxed to drive back to Mexico City after their elaborate meals.

\$\$ La Strada. For a change from Mexican food, come to this old-timer to enjoy a good Italian meal on a colonial candlelit patio. You can't go wrong with the fish dishes, pizzas (ask for the pizza menu), or the house beef specialty—*filete de Estrada*, served with homemade pasta. A guitarist plays Wednesday and Friday night, and the chef whips up weekend specials each Friday. *Salazar 3, around corner from Palacio de Cortés, tel. 73/18–60–85.* AE, MC, V.

\$ Vienes. Founded by an Austrian several generations ago, this Austro-Hungarian restaurant—which has grown up with the town—serves excellent Wiener schnitzel and goulash and irresistible pastries such as Sacher torte and apple strudel. *Lerdo de Tejada 302, at Comonfort, 1 block west of main square, tel. 73/14–34–04.* AE, MC, V.

\$\$\$\$–\$\$\$ Las Mañanitas. Opened 41 years ago by an American expat, rooms and suites here are exquisitely decorated with traditional Mexican fireplaces, hand-carved bedsteads, hand-painted tiles in the bathrooms, and gilded handicrafts. Mexico City residents drive an hour on weekends just to dine at the restaurant, with its spectacular open-air terraces and garden inhabited by flamingos, peacocks, and African cranes. Portions are ample, as with the tried-and-true favorite Mexican Plate—enchilada, chile relleno, *carne asada* (thinly sliced oven-grilled beef), and tamale, served with side dishes of guacamole and refried beans. Don't miss the black-bottom (chocolate) pie. *Ricardo Linares 107, 62000, tel. 73/14–14–66, fax 73/18–36–72. 1 room, 22 suites. Restaurant, bar, pool.* AE.

\$\$\$ Camino Real Sumiya. The romantic hideaway, built by Woolworth heiress Barbara Hutton, was converted into a restaurant after she died. In 1993 new owners took over and turned it into a posh hotel. It's set amid formal Japanese gardens (including a contemplative rock garden) and contains an original Kabuki theater brought over from Kyoto. A concierge takes care of every need. The rooms, which are equipped with modern furniture, two queen-size beds, and color satellite TVs, are set in the far part of the garden for privacy. Nonguests can eat in the restaurant. *Morelos 62550, about 15 mins south of town at Interior del Fracc. Sumiya, Col. José Parres, Juitepec (take Civac exit on Acapulco Hwy.), tel. 73/20–91–99, 800/722–6466 in the U.S. and Canada, fax 73/20–91–42. 163 rooms. 2 restaurants, bar, coffee shop, pool, 7 tennis courts, travel services. AE, DC, MC, V.*

$$$ Clarion Cuernavaca Racquet Club. This posh tennis club–turned–hotel is less expensive than most lodgings, and its appeal is in its beautiful gardens and spacious two-room suites equipped with romantic fireplaces. Families converge here on weekends. The restaurant admits nonguests. *Francisco Villa 100, Rancho Cortés, 62120, tel. 73/11–24–00, 800/228–5151 in the U.S. and Canada, fax 73/17–54–83. 52 suites. Restaurant, bar, pool, 9 tennis courts. AE, DC, MC, V.*

$$ Hacienda de Cortés. This old hacienda dates from the 16th century and did belong to the conquistador. Rooms are decorated in traditional Mexican furnishings; they have lovely patios and gardens that will beckon you outdoors, as well as TVs and minibars inside. *Plaza Kennedy 90, Col. Atlacomulco, 62250, tel. 73/15–88–44, fax 73/15–00–35. 22 rooms. Restaurant, bar, pool. AE, MC, V.*

$$ Hotel Jacarandas. Another former hacienda close to the downtown area, this hotel has the open, luxurious feel of an old-time Cuernavaca ranch. Huge laurel and fruit trees, jacarandas (of course), and poinsettias fill out the hotel's 98,000 square ft of terraced gardens, as do three pools, two tennis courts, and herb and vegetable gardens the hotel restaurant uses for its salads and herbal teas. This is a popular spot among Mexico City families. The rooms are simple, with TVs but no cable. *Cuauhtémoc 33, Col. Chapultepec, 62450, tel. 73/15–77–77, fax 73/15–78–88. 80 rooms, 6 suites. Restaurant, bar, 3 pools, 2 tennis courts, squash. AE, DC, MC, V.*

SOUTH OF MEXICO CITY A TO Z
Arriving and Departing

To get to **Xochimilco** by car, take Periférico Sur to the extension of División del Norte. Xochimilco is 21 km (13 mi) from the Zócalo in Mexico City; the trip should take between 45 minutes and one hour, depending on traffic. If Xochimilco is your final stop, you are probably best off taking a taxi. By public transportation, take metro line No. 2 to Taxqueña and then any bus marked Xochimilco.

To continue south by car, return to Periférico Sur, turn left (south) on Viaducto Tlalpán, and watch for signs to **Cuernavaca** in about a half hour. The *cuota* (toll road, Route 95D) costs about $6 but is much faster than the *carretera libre* (free road, Route 95). On Route 95D, it will take you about 1¼ hours to cover 85 km (53 mi).

Contacts and Resources

E-MAIL
The **Export Internet Café** (Av. Morelos Sur 168, Local A–6, near the state tourist office, tel. 73/12–16–56) is open daily 10–7 and charges $3 an hour.

VISITOR INFORMATION
The **Morelos State Tourist Office** (Av. Morelos Sur 187, tel. 73/14–38–72) in Cuernavaca is located in Colonia Las Palmas; it's open weekdays 8–3 and 6–9, weekends 9–2.

SOUTHEAST OF MEXICO CITY

Well-preserved colonial Puebla was once the center of the Spanish tile industry. On the way out of Mexico City, you'll see the volcanoes, Popocatépetl (pronounced poh-poh-kah-*teh*-pettle) and Iztaccíhuatl (pronounced eesh-tah-*see*-wattle). On your way back, leave time—an entire day would be best—to visit the city of Tlaxcala, with its rare church and former convent, and an amazing archaeological site nearby.

PUEBLA

Maize was first cultivated in the Tehuacán Valley around 5000 BC. Later, the region was a crossroads for many ancient Mesoamerican cultures, including the Olmecs and Totonacs. The young Spanish colony Puebla had the first glass factory, the first textile mill, and the second hospital. The battle of May 5, 1862—resulting in a short-lived victory against French invaders—took place just north of town. The national holiday, Cinco de Mayo, is celebrated yearly on that date in its honor, and the battle is reenacted.

Puebla today retains a strong conservative religious element and was one of the cities Pope John Paul II chose to visit during his 1978 Mexican tour. Overrun with religious structures, this city probably has more ex-convents and monasteries, chapels, and churches per square mile than anywhere else in the country. In fact, the valley of Puebla, which includes Cholula, was said to have 224 churches and 10 convents and monasteries in its heyday.

The city is full of idiosyncratic Baroque structures built with red bricks, gray stone, white stucco, and the beautiful Talavera tiles produced from local clay. Puebla is one of the few cities in Mexico declared a Patrimony of Humanities site by the United Nations because of the splendor of its colonial architecture.

Don't miss the **cathedral** (Calle 2 Sur, south of the Zócalo), partially financed by Puebla's most famous son, Bishop Juan de Palafox y Mendoza—who donated his personal fortune to build its famous tower, the second-largest church tower in the country. Palafox was the illegitimate son of a Spanish nobleman who grew up poor but inherited his father's wealth. Onyx, marble, and gold adorn the cathedral's high altar, designed by Mexico's most illustrious colonial architect, Manuel Tolsá. The facade itself is gray and cheerless.

The **Iglesia de Santo Domingo** (Santo Domingo Church; Av. Cinco de Mayo at Av. 4 Pte.) is especially famous for its Rosary

Chapel, where almost every inch of the walls, ceilings, and altar is covered with gilded carvings and sculpture.

The **Museo Amparo,** filled with the private collection of pre-Columbian and colonial art of Mexican banker and philanthropist Manuel Espinoza Yglesias, is one of the most beautiful in Mexico. *Calle 2 Sur at Av. 9 Ote., tel. 2/246–46–46. $1.60, free Mon. Wed.–Mon. 10–6.*

The **Uriarte Talavera** pottery factory was founded in 1824 and is one of the few authentic Talavera workshops left today. To be authentic, the pieces must be hand-painted in intricate designs with natural dyes derived from minerals, which is why only five colors are used: blue, black, yellow, green, and a reddish pink. There is a shop on site, and free tours of the factory run Monday through Saturday 10–2. *Av. 4 Pte. 911, between Avs. 9 and 11 Nte., tel. 2/232–15–98. Weekdays 9–6:30, Sat. 10–6:30, Sun. 11–6.*

Visit the **Barrio del Artista** (Calle 8 Nte. and Av. 6 Ote.) to watch painters and sculptors working in the galleries 10–6 daily. You may purchase pieces here, or continue walking down Calle 8 Norte and buy Talavera pottery, cheaper copies of Talavera, and other local handicrafts from the dozens of small stores and street vendors along the way.

The colonial **Ex-Convento de Santa Rosa,** now a museum of native crafts, contains the intricately tiled kitchen where Puebla's renowned mole sauce is believed to have been invented by the nuns as a surprise for their demanding gourmet bishop. *Av. 14 Pte. between Calles 3 and 5 Nte., tel. 2/246–22–71. 40¢.*

Puebla is also famous for *camote,* a popular candy made from sweet potatoes and fruit. **La Calle de las Dulces** (Sweets Street; Av. 6 Ote. between Av. 5 de Mayo and Calle 4 Nte.) is lined with shops competing to sell a wide variety of freshly made camote.

Dining and Lodging

Puebla is noted for its cuisine—some consider it to be the best in the country. Two of Mexico's most popular dishes were created here to celebrate special occasions: mole, a sauce made with as many as 100 ingredients, the best-known mole being one with bitter chocolate. The other local specialty, believed to have been initiated by the town's nuns, is *chiles en nogada*, a green poblano chili filled with ground meats, fruits, and nuts, then covered with a sauce of chopped walnuts and cream, and topped with red pomegranate seeds; the colors represent the red, green, and white of the Mexican flag.

\$\$ Las Bodegas del Molino. In a 16th-century hacienda at the edge of town, this elegant restaurant is notable for both its setting and its fine cuisine. *Molino de San José del Puente, tel. 22/49–04–83 or 22/49–06–51. No credit cards.*

\$ Fonda Santa Clara. This popular spot is a favorite among travelers; it's only a few blocks from the Zócalo and is open for breakfast, lunch, and dinner. *Calle 3 Pte. 307, tel. 22/42–26–59. AE, MC, V.*

\$ La Guadalupana. Puebla's most talked-about restaurant is a good choice for lunch. You'll find typical Poblano dishes on the menu. *Av. 5 Ote. 605, at Plazuela de los Sapos (Plaza of the Frogs), tel. 22/42–48–86. V.*

\$\$–\$\$\$ Mesón Sacristia de la Companía. Each room in this reconditioned 200-year-old town house is outfitted with antiques that you can purchase. The restaurant serves everything from steaks to the scrumptious "Grandma's enchiladas." *Calle 6 Sur 304, at Callejón de los Sapos, 72000, tel. 22/32–45–13. 9 rooms. Restaurant, bar. AE, MC, V.*

\$\$\$ Camino Real. The accommodations are deluxe in this former 16th-century convent, with gilded antique furnishings, luminous restored fresco murals, and an exceptionally warm and professional staff. *Av. 7 Pte. 105, 72000, tel. 22/29–09–09, 22/29–09–10, 800/722–6466, fax 22/32–92–51. 83 rooms. Restaurant, bar, in-room data ports, business services. AE, DC, MC, V.*

$$$ **El Mesón del Angel.** At the city's entrance is this quiet colonial hotel with two large gardens. It's peaceful and clean, though a bit far from the attractions. *Av. Hermanos Serdan 807, 72100, tel. 22/23–83–01. 192 rooms. Restaurant, 2 bars, pool, business services. AE, MC, V.*

$$ **Royalty.** Small and well maintained, this hotel on the main square is one of the less expensive choices in Puebla. *Portal Hidalgo 8, 72000, tel. 22/42–47–40. 47 rooms. Restaurant, bar. MC, V.*

TLAXCALA

The warriors of the state of Tlaxcala (pronounced tlas-*ca*-la) played a pivotal role in the Spanish conquest by aligning themselves with Cortés against their enemy Aztecs, thus swelling the conqueror's military ranks by 5,000 men. The state capital, seat of the ancient nation with the same name, will interest both archaeology buffs and church lovers.

A former Franciscan church, now called the **Catedral de Nuestro Señora de la Asunción** (Our Lady of the Assumption Cathedral), with its adjoining **monastery** (1537–40), stands atop a hill one block from the handsome main square. This was the first permanent Catholic edifice in the New World. The most unusual feature of the church is its wood ceiling beams, carved and gilded with gold studs after the Moorish fashion. There are only three churches of this kind in Mexico. (Moorish, or mudéjar, architecture appeared in Mexico only during the very early years after the conquest, when the Moorish occupation was still recent enough to influence Spain with Arabic architectural styles.) The austere monastery, now a museum of history, displays 16th- and 18th-century religious paintings and a small collection of pre-Columbian pieces. A beautiful outdoor **chapel** near the monastery has notable Moorish and Gothic traces.

The **Palacio de Gobierno** (Government Palace), which occupies the north side of the Zócalo, was built about 1550. Inside are vivid epic murals of Tlaxcala before the conquest, painted in the 1960s by local artist Desiderio Hernández Xochitiotzin.

About 1 km (½ mi) west of Tlaxcala is the large, ornate **Santuario de la Virgen de Ocotlán** (Basilica of Our Lady of Ocotlán). The legend of the Virgin dates from 1541, when, during a severe epidemic, she appeared to a poor Indian and told him to take the water from a stream, which had miraculously appeared, to his people to cure them. The villagers recovered. The Virgin then asked for the Franciscan monks from a nearby monastery. When they arrived in her forest, they were temporarily blinded by the raging flames of a fire that didn't harm the trees. They returned the next day with an axe to cut open one particular pine (*ocotlán*) tree that had caught their attention. When they split it open, they discovered the wooden image of the Virgin, which they installed in the present basilica. Many miracles have been attributed to the Virgin since then. Noteworthy sights of the church are the churrigueresque white-plaster facade, which conjures up images of a wedding cake; the two white Poblano towers adorned with the apostles; and, inside, the brilliantly painted and gilded **Camarín de la Virgen** (Virgin's Dressing Room) with figures on each of its eight sides portraying the history of the Lady of Ocotlán.

SOUTHEAST OF MEXICO CITY A TO Z
Getting Around

BY CAR

From Mexico City, head east on the Viaducto Miguel Aleman toward the airport and exit right onto Calzada Zaragoza, the last wide boulevard before arriving at the airport; this becomes the Puebla Highway at the tollbooth. Route 150D is the toll road straight to **Puebla**; Route 190 is the scenic free road. The trip takes about 1¼ hours on the former, three hours on the latter.

Contacts and Resources

E-MAIL
The **Cyberbyte Café** (Calle 2 Sur 505B, between Avs. 5 and 7 Ote., Puebla, tel. 22/17–55–23) is open daily 10–9 and charges $2.50 an hour.

VISITOR INFORMATION
The **Puebla Tourist Office** (Av. 5 Ote. 3, tel. 22/46–12–85) is open Monday–Saturday 9–8, Sunday 9–2. Ask for Jorge Estrada or Jose Luis Hernández; both speak English and love to talk up their state.

WEST OF MEXICO CITY

A good weekend destination west of Mexico City is Valle de Bravo, a lovely lakeside village popular with vacationing chilangos; it's often called Mexico's Switzerland because of its green, hilly setting.

VALLE DE BRAVO

In colonial Valle de Bravo, white stucco houses are trimmed with wrought-iron balconies and red-tile roofs, and red-potted succulents clutter the doorways. A hilly town that rises from the shores of Lake Avandaro and is surrounded by pines and mountains, Valle was founded in 1530 but has no historical monuments to speak of other than the town church. It does, however, have plenty of diversions: boating, waterskiing, and swimming in the lake and its waterfalls, and the more sociable pleasures of the Sunday market, where exceptional pottery is the draw. Although Valle and its suburb of Avandaro are enclaves for artists and the wealthy, locals like to keep a low profile.

Lodging

$$$ Avandaro Golf & Spa Resort. For a weekend stay, head for this posh former country club, where all the rooms have romantic fireplaces. In addition to its 18-hole golf course, the resort has one of the best high-tech spas in Mexico, equipped with hot tubs and offering massage, facials, body toning, and aerobics classes. *Vega del Río, Fracc. Avandaro, 52100, tel. 726/6–03–66, 800/ 223–6510, fax 726/6–09–05. 74 rooms. Restaurant, bar, pool, spa, 18-hole golf course, health club. AE, MC, V.*

WEST OF MEXICO CITY A TO Z
Getting There

There are two choices for getting to **Valle de Bravo:** the winding, scenic route, which you pick up 3 km (2 mi) west of Zincantepec, or Route 15. The former takes twice as much time but is worth it for the unspoiled mountain scenery.

Visitor Information

The **Mexico State Tourist Office** (Urawa 100, Gate 110, Toluca, tel. 72/19–51–90 or 72/19–61–58) is open weekdays 9–6.

In This Chapter

Updated by Patricia Alisau

where to stay

ALTHOUGH THE CITY IS HUGE and spread out, most hotels are within a relatively manageable group of neighborhoods. Stylish Colonia Polanco and Bosque de Chapultepec are on the west side of the city. Paseo de la Reforma runs from Chapultepec, northeast through "midtown," and intersects with Avenida Juárez at the beginning of the downtown area. Juárez becomes Calle Madero, which continues east to the downtown historic district and its very core, the Zócalo. The Zona Rosa, replete with boutiques, cafés, restaurants, and nightspots, is literally across Reforma (south), in the western midtown area.

Business travelers tend to fill up deluxe hotels during the week; some major hotels discount their weekend rates. If you reserve through the toll-free reservations numbers, you probably will find rates as much as 50% off during special promotions. You can expect hotels in the $$$ and $$$$ categories to have purified water, air-conditioning, cable TV, radio, minibars, and extended (often 24-hour) room service.

CATEGORY	COST*
$$$$	over $160
$$$	$90–$160
$$	$40–$90
$	under $40

*All prices are for a standard double room, excluding service charge and 15% sales tax. There is an additional 2% room tax.

COLONIA POLANCO AND BOSQUE DE CHAPULTEPEC

$$$$ CAMINO REAL. ★ About the size of the Teotihuacán's Pyramid of the Sun, this sleek, minimalist, bright pink and yellow, 8-acre city-within-a-city attracts everyone from heads of state and celebrities to holiday travelers. Impressive works of art embellishing the endless corridors and lounges include Rufino Tamayo's mural *Man Facing Infinity* and a Calder sculpture. The fifth-floor executive level has 100 extra-large guest rooms with special amenities. Fouquet's de Paris restaurant (☞ Eating Out) holds culinary events, and the airy Azulejos serves Mexican fare and Sunday buffet brunches. A nightclub hosts top Latin American artists who perform Thursday through Saturday starting at 11 PM; there's dancing after the show. *Mariano Escobedo 700, 11590, tel. 5/203–2121, 800/722–6466, fax 5/250–6897, 5/250–6723. 673 rooms, 36 suites. 3 restaurants, 4 bars, pool, 4 tennis courts, health club, nightclub, business services. AE, DC, MC, V. www.caminoreal.com/mexicocity*

$$$$ CASA VIEJA. This classically elegant, sumptuously decorated Colonia Polanco mansion is the dream-come-true of a local businessman who took his love of things Mexican and expressed it in his all-suites (one and two bedrooms) hotel. Tastefully selected folk art, handsomely hand-carved furniture, and gilded wall trimmings complement patios and splashing fountains. Lively Mexican colors are a light-hearted touch in the 10 suites, all of them different. All have a full kitchen, fax machine, CD and video-cassette players, hot tub, and picture window overlooking an inside garden. The hotel's Mexican restaurant is named after its huge floor-to-ceiling *Arbor de la Vida* (Tree of Life) sculpture. Rates include breakfast. *Eugenio Sue 45, Col. Polanco, 11560, tel. 5/282–0067, fax 5/281–3780. 10 suites. Restaurant, bar, concierge, free parking. AE, MC, V.*

$$$$ J. W. MARRIOTT. In posh Colonia Polanco, this hotel was designed as a boutique property with personalized service and small, clubby public areas; nothing overwhelms here. Rooms are done with plenty of wood and warm colors but are otherwise unremarkable in decor. Each has a work desk with an outlet for a personal computer and modem. The hotel has the best-equipped business center in the city, open 24 hours. Executive floors come with extra amenities. The pretty Thai House restaurant is also on site. *Andrés Bello 29, at Campos Elíseos, Col. Polanco, 11560, tel. 5/282–8888, 800/228–9290, fax 5/282–8811. 312 rooms. 3 restaurants, bar, coffee shop, pool, exercise room, business services, meeting rooms, travel services, car rental. AE, DC, MC, V. www.marriotthotels.com*

$$$$ NIKKO MÉXICO. Part of the Japanese Nikko chain, this glistening, 42-floor high-rise occupies a prime Polanco position: adjacent to Bosque de Chapultepec, just a five-minute walk from the Anthropology Museum. It has signage and menus in Japanese, English, and Spanish. Although it's the second-largest hotel in the city and has marvelous views from the top floor, its standard rooms are a little claustrophobic; executive floors have better rooms and extra facilities. Four top restaurants excel in their gastronomic specialties: Les Célébrités (International) (☞ Eating Out), Teppan Grill and Benkay (both Japanese), and El Jardín (international). The cozy Shelty's Pub is also a big hit with locals. *Campos Elíseos 204, 11560, tel. 5/280–1111, 01–800/908–8800, 800/645–5687 in the U.S. and Canada, fax 5/280–9191. 724 rooms, 24 suites. 4 restaurants, 2 bars, indoor pool, 4 tennis courts, health club, jogging, dance club, business services, meeting rooms, travel services, car rental. AE, DC, MC, V. www.nikkohotels.com*

$$$$ PRESIDENTE INTER-CONTINENTAL MÉXICO. This 42-story Inter-Continental, adjacent to Bosque de Chapultepec in Colonia Polanco, has a dramatic five-story atrium lobby—a hollow pyramid of balconies—with music performed daily at the lively lobby bar. Rooms are spacious, and all have work areas. On clear days, the top two floors have views of the nearby snowcapped volcanoes. The executive floors have a lounge,

mexico city lodging

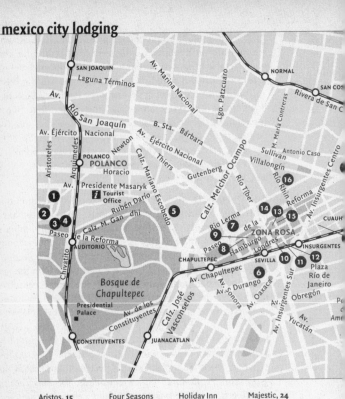

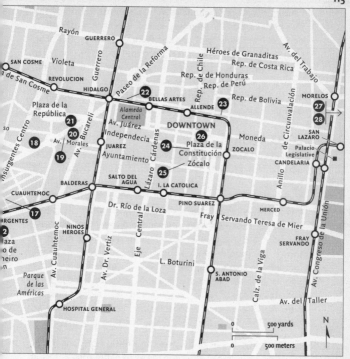

Marriott Aeropuerto, **27**

Meliá México Reforma, **21**

Misión Park Plaza México, **17**

Nikko México, **4**

Plaza Florencia, **10**

Presidente Inter-Continental México, **3**

Sevilla Palace, **18**

concierge, and extra amenities. A number of smart stores and six eateries are on the premises, including branches of Maxim's de Paris (☞ Eating Out) and the Palm and Alfredo Di Roma. *Campos Elíseos 218, 11560, tel. 5/327–7700, 800/327–0200 in the U.S. and Canada, fax 5/327–7730. 627 rooms, 32 suites. 6 restaurants, coffee shop, lobby lounge, exercise room, baby-sitting, business services, meeting rooms, travel services, car rental, parking (fee). AE, DC, MC, V. www.interconti.com*

ZONA ROSA

$$$$ **GALERÍA PLAZA.** Part of the Westin Hotel deluxe chain, this
★ ultramodern property is on a quiet street in elegant Zona Rosa—ideal for shopping, enjoying nightlife, and dining out. Standard rooms are relatively small, but service and facilities are faultless. Rooms on the executive floor, where a special concierge desk provides personalized service and easy checkout, are larger. Other advantages include voice mail in all rooms, a heated rooftop pool with sundeck, a secure underground parking lot, and a 24-hour restaurant, which has a popular buffet breakfast. *Hamburgo 195, at Varsovia, 06600, tel. 5/ 208–0370, 800/228–3000, fax 5/207–5867. 420 rooms, 19 suites. 3 restaurants, lobby lounge, room service, pool, exercise room, concierge, travel services, parking (fee). AE, DC, MC, V. www.westin.com*

$$$$ **KRYSTAL ROSA.** Part of the Mexican Krystal Hotel chain, this superbly run high-rise hotel is in the heart of the Zona Rosa and has an excellent view of the city from the rooftop pool terrace. There is a stylish lobby cocktail lounge, a bar with local entertainers, and a restaurant, Hacienda del Mortero, that serves excellent classic Mexican cuisine. Two club floors have VIP check-in and service, complimentary Continental buffet breakfast, and rooms with extra amenities. *Liverpool 155, 06600, tel. 5/228–9928, fax 5/228–9929. 267 rooms, 35 suites. 2 restaurants, 2 bars, pool, concierge, business services, parking (fee). AE, DC, MC, V.*

$$$ ARISTOS. On bustling Paseo de la Reforma a few blocks east of the U.S. Embassy and near the Mexican Stock Exchange, this 15-story Zona Rosa–fringe hotel wears its age well (it was one of the first luxury hotels in the area). Rooms are well supplied and attractively decorated in shades of peach and mauve, with brass and wood accents. The business center has a bilingual staff and a message service. *Paseo de la Reforma 276, 06600, tel. 5/211–0112, fax 5/514–3543. 298 rooms, 29 suites. 4 restaurants, bar, beauty salon, sauna, exercise room, travel services, parking (fee). AE, DC, MC, V.*

$$$ CALINDA GENEVE. A Quality Inn, referred to locally as El Génova, this five-story 1906 hotel is fitted with traditional colonial-style carved wood chairs and tables in the pleasant lobby; guest rooms are smallish but comfortable. The hotel's attraction as a gathering place has always been the Salón Jardín, a striking Belle Epoque gallery with a profusion of plants and a high stained-glass ceiling; it's been taken over by the popular Sanborns restaurant chain with little change to its decor. The hotel's informal street-front Café Jardín serves until 10 PM, and a branch of the Sanborns retail chain, which sells sundries, opens off the lobby. *Londres 130, 06600, tel. 5/211–0071, 800/228–5151, fax 5/208–7422. 320 rooms. Restaurant, bar, café, room service, exercise room, coin laundry, business services. AE, DC, MC, V. www.hotelchoice.com*

$$$ LA CASONA. This elegant, understated mansion, registered as an artistic monument by Mexico's Institute of Fine Arts, was turned into a charming 30-room hotel in 1996. Filled with sunny patios and sitting rooms, the hotel is finely decorated with antiques, expensive rugs, hardwood floors, and accessories in the spirit of the days of the Porfiriato, when the house was built. No two rooms are alike, but all have hair dryers, fluffy bathrobes and slippers, and good-size bathtubs. There's a small restaurant that serves old-style country cooking. The two-story hotel building, with its demure salmon facade, looks out on a tree-lined street in Colonia Roma, about a 10-minute walk south of the Zona Rosa and in easy reach of museums, restaurants, and Paseo de la Reforma. A Continental breakfast is included in the price of a room. *Durango 280, at Cozumel, tel. 5/286–3001, 800/ 223–5652, fax 5/211–0871. 30 rooms. Restaurant, bar, room service, exercise room. AE, DC, MC, V. www.yellow.com.mx/casona*

$$$ MARCO POLO. Ultramodern and intimate, the central Zona
★ Rosa all-suites Marco Polo has the amenities and outstanding personalized service often associated with a small European hotel. All rooms have climate control, cable TV, FM radio, minibar, and work desks; some suites have hot tubs. North-facing top-floor rooms have excellent views of Paseo de la Reforma and the Angel monument—the four penthouse suites have terraces—and the U.S. Embassy is close by. In the street-level Bistro de Marco Polo, you can listen to sophisticated piano music evenings 7–9. *Amberes 27, 06600, tel. 5/207–1893, fax 5/ 533–3727. 60 suites. Restaurant, bar, business services. AE, DC, MC, V. www.marcopolo.com.mx*

$$$ PLAZA FLORENCIA. This modern hotel is on a busy avenue that borders the Zona Rosa—and the low end of $$$. The lobby's heavy furniture and dark colors make it feel more like a lodge, in which guests relax after a day of exploring. Rooms are well furnished in hotel-modern style—cheerfully decorated, and soundproofed against the location's heavy traffic noise; higher floors have views of the Angel monument. Some large family suites are available. All rooms have air-conditioning, heat, color TV, and a phone. A business center offers fax, copy, computer, and Internet-access services. *Florencia 61, 06600, tel. 5/211–0064, fax 5/511–1542. 130 rooms, 12 suites. Restaurant, bar, coffee shop, business services. AE, DC, MC, V. www.florencia.web.com.mx*

$$ MISIÓN PARK PLAZA MÉXICO. A part of the Misión chain, this very comfortable hotel a few blocks from the Zona Rosa's eastern end is well placed for shopping and sightseeing. Mirrors, good light, and like-new bathrooms make the rooms more pleasant; all have air-conditioning and color TV with U.S. channels. Sixteen rooms have been converted into executive units that have work areas, and Internet connection has been added to an office off the lobby for guests' use. Staff is friendly and accommodating, and breakfast is included in the room rates. *Napoles 62, 06600, tel. 5/533–0535, fax 5/533–1589. 50 rooms. Coffee shop, lobby lounge, exercise room, meeting rooms. AE, MC, V. www.hotelesmision.com.mx*

MIDTOWN AND ALONG THE REFORMA

$$$$ FOUR SEASONS MEXICO CITY. This is—perhaps by definition—
★ one of the most luxurious hotels in the capital and accordingly has won the AAA Five Diamond Award three years running. Surrounding a traditional courtyard with a fountain, the eight-story building was modeled after the 18th-century Iturbide Palace downtown. Half the rooms overlook the lush inner courtyard garden. Huge bowls of flowers and lovely European furnishings fill the spacious marble lobby. Geared for business travelers, rooms have data ports and all the amenities you'd expect at a Four Seasons hotel. There's also a boardroom on the premises and a full-service business center with even a reference library. A well-stocked tequila bar off the lobby is a perfect pre-dinner option. Excellent cultural tours of the city are offered free to guests on weekends. *Paseo de la Reforma 500, 06600, tel. 5/230–1818, 800/332–3442, fax 5/230–1808. 200 rooms, 40 suites. 2 restaurants, 2 bars, pool, exercise room, health club, business services, meeting rooms. AE, DC, MC, V. www.fourseasons.com*

$$$$ MARÍA ISABEL SHERATON. Don Antenor Patiño, the Bolivian "Tin King," inaugurated this Mexico City classic in 1969 and named it after his granddaughter, socialite Isabel Goldsmith. The hotel is constantly being remodeled, but the glistening brown marble and Art Deco details in the lobby and other public areas remain. All guest and public rooms are impeccably maintained; penthouse suites in the 22-story tower section are extra-spacious and exceptionally luxurious. The location— across from the Angel monument and the Zona Rosa, with Sanborns next door and the U.S. Embassy a half block away—is prime. It has the largest conference room (for 1,500) in town. *Paseo de la Reforma 325, 06500, tel. 5/207–3933, 800/334–8484, fax 5/207–0684. 681 rooms, 74 suites. 3 restaurants, bar, room service, pool, massage, sauna, health club, concierge floor, business services, meeting rooms, parking (fee). AE, DC, MC, V. www.sheraton.com*

$$$$ **MARQUIS REFORMA.** Opened in 1991, this plush, privately
★ owned member of the Leading Hotels of the World, and 1999 recipient of the Five Stars and Five Diamonds Award given by the Mexican government, is within walking distance of the Zona Rosa. It has a striking pink-stone and curved-glass Art Nouveau facade, and its seventh-floor suites afford picture-perfect views of the Castillo de Chapultepec. The elegant lobby is fitted in a classic European style, with paintings, sculpture, and palatial furniture. Guest-room furniture and decor are Art Deco–inspired. The award-winning La Jolla restaurant serves Mexican cuisine. The fully staffed corporate center has state-of-the-art computer services, and guest-room phones feature a second plug for computers with fax modem. The health club has hard-to-find holistic, stress-busting massages. *Paseo de la Reforma 465, 06500, tel. 5/211–3600, 800/235–2387, 877/818–5011 in Canada, fax 5/211– 5561. 133 rooms, 84 suites. 2 restaurants, bar, health club, business services, meeting room. AE, DC, MC, V. www.hotelmarquisrsma.com.mx*

$$$$ **MELÍA MÉXICO REFORMA.** Perched at the junction of Paseo de la Reforma, Juárez, and Bucareli—convenient to downtown, the Zona Rosa, and the Stock Exchange—this flashy 22-story smoked-glass behemoth (formerly part of the Crowne Plaza chain) looks quite spectacular in its otherwise nondescript surroundings. It touts the ultimate in high-tech amenities for business travelers: a stock-market indicator, computers, cellular phones, and secretarial, translation, messenger, and shipping services. Executive rooms have PC- and fax-modem

© 2000 Visa U.S.A. Inc.

When it Comes to Getting Local Currency at an ATM, Same Thing.

Whether you're in Yosemite or Yemen, using your Visa® card or ATM card with the PLUS symbol is the easiest and most convenient way to get local currency. For example, let's say you're in France. When you make a withdrawal, using your secured PIN, it's dispensed in francs, but is debited from your account in U.S. dollars. This makes it easy to take advantage of favorable exchange rates. And if you need help finding one of Visa's 627,000 ATMs in 127 countries worldwide, visit **visa.com/pd/atm**. We'll make finding an ATM as easy as finding the Eiffel Tower, the Pyramids or even the Grand Canyon.

It's Everywhere You Want To Be®

SEE THE WORLD
IN FULL COLOR

Fodor's Exploring Guides bring all the great sights vividly to life with hundreds of photographs, fascinating historical background, and colorful anecdotes. Detailed maps and practical information keep you headed in the right direction.

Pair a Fodor's Exploring Guide with your trusted Fodor's Pocket Guide for a complete planning package.

Fodor's EXPLORING GUIDES

At bookstores everywhere.

outlets and three telephone lines. Public areas include a coffee bar with 20 java concoctions, an oyster-and-jazz bar, and a French restaurant. The hotel also has limousine rental, a pharmacy, and boutiques. *Paseo de la Reforma 1, Col. Tabacalera, 06030, tel. 5/128–5000, 800/336–3542, fax 5/128–5050. 424 rooms, 30 suites. 2 restaurants, 2 bars, room service, beauty salon, shops, business services, travel services, car rental. AE, DC, MC, V.*

$$$ FIESTA AMERICANA REFORMA. This immense hotel, built in the 1970s by a Mexican chain that billed it a "bar with a hotel," may be past its prime, but the business travelers and large groups that parade in and out of the lobby still keep it lively. There isn't much Mexican atmosphere except for the live Mexican music in the lobby bar, but there's something to say for being able to get a good tan on the sundeck, work out in the gym, and choose from two restaurants, one of which offers breakfast and lunch buffets. *Paseo de la Reforma 80, 06600, tel. 5/705–1515, 800/343–7821, fax 5/705–1313. 610 rooms. 2 restaurants, 2 bars, exercise room, business services, free parking. AE, DC, MC, V. www.fiestaamericana.com*

$$ IMPERIAL. Opened in 1990, the Imperial occupies a stately late-19th-century European-style building right on the Reforma alongside the Columbus Monument. Quiet elegance and personal service are keynotes of this privately owned property. The hotel's Restaurant Gaudí has an understated, tony atmosphere and serves Continental cuisine with some classic Spanish selections. All rooms have safes. *Paseo de la Reforma 64, 06600, tel. 5/705–4911, fax 5/703–3122. 50 rooms, 10 junior suites, 5 master suites. Restaurant, bar, café, business services, meeting rooms, travel services. AE, DC, MC, V. www.hotelimperial.com.mx*

$$ MARÍA CRISTINA. Full of old-world charm, this Spanish colonial-★ style gem is a Mexico City classic. Impeccably maintained since it was built in 1937 (it was last refurbished in January 1995), the building surrounds a delightful garden courtyard—the setting for its El Retiro bar. Three tastefully decorated apartment-style master suites, complete with hot tubs, were added in the early '90s. All rooms have safes. Located in a quiet residential setting near Parque Sullivan, the hotel is a block from the Paseo de la Reforma and close to the Zona Rosa. *Río Lerma 31, 06500, tel. 5/ 566–9688, fax 5/566–9194. 140 rooms, 8 suites. Bar, room service, beauty salon, travel services. MC, V.*

$$ SEVILLA PALACE. This glistening modern showplace has five panoramic elevators for its 23 floors, a covered rooftop pool with hot tub, a health club, a top-floor supper club with entertainment, a terraced rooftop lounge with a city view, and convention halls with capacities of up to 1,000. It's near the Columbus traffic circle and attracts lots of tourists from Spain. *Paseo de la Reforma 105, 06030, tel. 5/705–2800, 800/732–9488, fax 5/703–1521. 413 rooms. 2 restaurants, 3 bars, pool, health club, nightclub, meeting rooms. AE, MC, V. www.sevillapalace.com.mx*

DOWNTOWN

$$$ MAJESTIC. The atmospheric, colonial-style Majestic, built in 1937, is perfectly located if you're interested in exploring the historic downtown: on the Zócalo at the corner of Madero. This Best Western property is also perfect for viewing the Independence Day (September 16) celebrations, which draw hundreds of thousands of people to this square, and many people reserve a room a year in advance of the festivities. Rooms are decorated in the style of the 1940s and have no air-conditioning but are kept cool by high ceilings and the fact that you are in a high-mountain city; each has a remote-control color TV and a minibar. Although the front units have balconies and a charming view, they can be noisy with car traffic until about 11 at night. Service is efficient and courteous. The seventh-floor La Terraza dining room and terrace—which serve international and Mexican specialties—have marvelous panoramas of the Zócalo. The Sunday buffet (1–5) features live Mexican music. The fun El Campanario piano bar welcomes anyone who wants to make a singing debut, and has become a favorite with locals. *Madero 73, 06000, tel. 5/521–8600, 800/528–1234, fax 5/512–6262. 85 rooms. Restaurant, bar, coffee shop, travel services. AE, DC, MC, V. www.bestwestern.com*

$$ GRAN HOTEL DE LA CIUDAD DE MÉXICO. Ensconced in what was formerly a 19th-century department store, this more traditional hotel has contemporary rooms. Its central location—adjacent to the Zócalo and near the Templo Mayor—makes it a good choice for local sightseeing. Its distinctive Belle Epoque lobby—with a striking stained-glass Tiffany dome, chandeliers, gilded birdcages, and 19th-century wrought-iron elevators—is worth a visit in its own right. The Mirador breakfast restaurant overlooks the Zócalo. The Del Centro restaurant-bar run by Delmónicos is one of Mexico City's best—a great place to stop for a drink while exploring nearby. The hotel has been undergoing a long-term, gradual refurbishing; be sure to request a renovated room that does not look out onto a brick wall. *16 de Septiembre 82, 06000, tel. 5/510–4040, fax 5/512–6772. 125 rooms. 2 restaurants, bar, concierge, travel services, parking (fee). AE, DC, MC, V.*

$$ HOLIDAY INN SELECT ZÓCALO. Opened in 1998, this hotel couldn't have a better location—on the Zócalo and close to a gaggle of museums, restaurants, and historic buildings. It's actually in a historic building that dates back to colonial times. The interior is modern and has the feel of a Holiday Inn. Although the glass-front lobby lacks personality, there's more flavor to the terrace restaurant, which is set with old-fashioned wrought-iron tables and has an amazing view of the Metropolitan Cathedral and National Palace. Rooms are small but well-equipped with closet safe, coffeemaker, air-conditioning and heat, iron and ironing board, and bathroom amenities. All suites have data ports; five have Jacuzzi bathtubs. *5 de Mayo at Zócalo, Centro Histórico, 06000, tel. 5/521–2121, 800/465–4329, fax 5/521–2122. 100 rooms, 15 suites. 2 restaurants, bar, room service, exercise room, meeting rooms, travel services, parking (fee). AE, MC, V. www.holiday-inn.com*

$$ HOTEL DE CORTÉS. This delightful small hotel, managed by Best Western, is housed in a 1780 colonial building that was designated a national monument. Colonial-decor rooms are small and simply furnished; they open onto an enclosed central courtyard. Two comfortable soundproof suites overlook Alameda Park across the busy street. A restaurant also looks onto the park, and a friendly bar opens to the tree-shaded central courtyard and fountain, a lovely setting for tea or cocktails. Friday evening at 7:30, there's a Mexican folkloric show with music and dance. The Franz Mayer Museum is just a block away, and it's an easy walk to Palacio de Bellas Artes. Loyal guests reserve many months in advance. *Av. Hidalgo 85, 06000, tel. 5/518–2184, 800/334–7234, fax 5/512–1863. 19 rooms, 10 suites. Restaurant, bar. AE, DC, MC, V. www.bestwestern.com*

$ CATEDRAL. ★ In the heart of historic downtown, this refurbished older hotel is a bargain, with many of the amenities of the more upscale hotels at less than half the price. Public areas sparkle with marble and glass. Guest rooms are done in a cheerful contemporary fashion, and all have color TVs (local channels only) and phones. You can get one with a view of the namesake Catedral, but keep in mind that its bells chime every 15 minutes late into the night. Service is friendly, the hotel restaurant is excellent, and El Retiro bar attracts a largely Mexican clientele to hear live Latin music. *Donceles 95, 06000, tel. 5/512–8581, fax 5/512–4344. 116 rooms. Bar, coffee shop, room service, nightclub, laundry service, dry cleaning, travel services. AE, MC, V.*

AIRPORT

$$$$ HILTON AEROPUERTO. This luxury oasis opened in 1998, marking the arrival of the only hotel inside the airport. Cool and compact, with a distinctive gray marble lobby and a wide-angle view from the bar of landing planes, the hotel feels like a private club with its subdued elegance and attentive but unobtrusive staff. Rooms come with full working gear for a traveling executive: two phone lines, modem connection, ergonomic chairs, and coffeemaker. Rooms have four different views—airstrip, street, atrium, or garden (bamboo plants set along a concrete ledge). All units wrap around one floor. *Benito Juárez International Airport, international terminal, 15520, tel. 5/133–0505, 800/445–8667, fax 5/133–0500. 129 rooms. Restaurant, bar, exercise room, business services, meeting room, parking (fee). AE, DC, MC, V. www.mexicocity.hilton.com*

$$$ MARRIOTT AEROPUERTO. Just over a short covered footbridge from the airport terminal is this deluxe hotel that's sleek and modern as well as comfortable. The hotel is convenient if you arrive late or have an early morning flight; you pay a price for this convenience, although discounted corporate rates are available. There's a pool on the eighth floor. Even if you're only between flights and don't overnight, you can sit in one of the overstuffed chairs in the soothing lobby to get away from the frantic energy of the airport, or catch a meal in the restaurant. *Benito Juárez International Airport, 15520, tel. 5/230–0505, 800/228–9290, fax 5/230–0555. 600 rooms, 8 suites. Restaurant, bar, coffee shop, pool, sauna, health club, meeting rooms, car rental, free parking. AE, DC, MC, V. www.marriotthotels.com*

PRACTICAL INFORMATION

Updated by Patricia Alisau and Paige Bierma

Air Travel

BOOKING

When you book **look for nonstop flights** and **remember that "direct" flights stop at least once.** Try to avoid connecting flights, which require a change of plane.

CARRIERS

All flights lead to Mexico City. Mexicana has scheduled service from Chicago, Denver, Los Angeles, Miami, New York, San Antonio, San Francisco, and San Jose. It has direct or connecting service at 30 locations throughout the country. Aeroméxico serves Mexico City daily from Dallas, Houston, Los Angeles, Miami, Orlando, New Orleans, Atlanta, New York, Phoenix, San Antonio, San Diego, and Tucson (as well as Tijuana). Aeroméxico serves some 35 cities within Mexico. Aerolitoral, a subsidiary of Aeroméxico based in Monterrey, serves north-central cities as well as San Antonio, Texas, via Monterrey from Mexico City. Taesa, a Mexican airline, has direct flights (but not nonstop) to Mexico City from Chicago and Oakland; directs and nonstops from Tijuana; and nonstops from Laredo, Texas.

North American carriers serving Mexico City include American, America West, Continental, Delta, Northwest, United, and US Airways. Air France flies nonstop between Houston and Mexico City.

➤ MAJOR AIRLINES: **American** (☎ 800/433–7300). **Continental** (☎ 800/231–0856). **Delta** (☎ 800/241–4141. **Northwest** (☎ 800/447–4747). **United** (☎ 800/241–6522). **US Airways** (☎ 800/428–4322).

➤ SMALLER AIRLINES: **AeroCalifornia** (☎ 800/237–6225). **Aeroméxico** (☎ 800/237–6639). **America West** (☎ 800/235–9292). **Mexicana** (☎ 800/531–7921).

➤ FROM THE U.K.: **British Airways** (☎ 0845/7733377) has a nonstop flight from London to Mexico City. Other airlines flying to Mexico, with brief stops en route, include **Air France** (☎ 020/8742–6600), via Paris; **American** (☎ 020/8572–5555, ☎ 0345/789789 outside London), from London via Chicago, Dallas, or Miami; **Continental** (☎ 01293/776464), from London via Houston, and from Birmingham and Manchester via Newark; **Delta** (☎ 0800/414767), via Atlanta; **Iberia** (☎ 020/7830–0011), via Madrid; **KLM** (☎ 020/8750–9820), via Amsterdam; **Lufthansa** (☎ 020/8750–3535), via Frankfurt; and **United** (☎ 020/8990–9900), via Chicago or Washington, D.C.

➤ DOMESTIC AIRLINES: **Aerocaribe** (reserve through Mexicana). **Aerolitoral** (reserve through Aeroméxico or Mexicana). **Aeromar** (reserve through Mexicana or Aeroméxico). **Aviacsa** (☎ 961/2–80–81 in Chiapas, 5/448–8900 in Mexico City). **Taesa** (☎ 5/227–0700, 800/328–2372).

CUTTING COSTS

The least expensive airfares to Mexico must usually be purchased in advance and are nonrefundable. It's smart to **call a number of airlines, and when you are quoted a good price, book it on the spot**—the same fare may not be available the next day. Always **check different routings** and look into using different airports. Travel agents, especially low-fare specialists, are helpful.

Consolidators are another good source. They buy tickets for scheduled international flights at reduced rates from the airlines, then sell them at prices that beat the best fare available directly from the airlines, usually without restrictions. Sometimes you can even get your money back if you need to return the ticket. Carefully read the fine print detailing penalties for changes and cancellations, and **confirm your consolidator reservation with the airline.**

➤ Consolidators: **Cheap Tickets** (☎ 800/377–1000). **Discount Airline Ticket Service** (☎ 800/576–1600). **Unitravel** (☎ 800/325–2222). **Up & Away Travel** (☎ 212/889–2345). **World Travel Network** (☎ 800/409–6753).

HOW TO COMPLAIN

If your baggage goes astray or your flight goes awry, complain right away. Most carriers require that you **file a claim** immediately.

➤ Airline Complaints: U.S. Department of Transportation **Aviation Consumer Protection Division** (✉ C-75, Room 4107, Washington, DC 20590, ☎ 202/366–2220, airconsumerost .dot.gov, www.dot.gov/airconsumer). **Federal Aviation Administration Consumer Hotline** (☎ 800/322–7873).

Airports & Transfers

The newest wing of Mexico City's **Aeropuerto Internacional Benito Juárez** is a high-tech, state-of-the-art elongation of the east end of the existing airport. Porters and free carts are available in the baggage-retrieval areas. Banks and currency exchanges rotate their schedules to provide around-the-clock service. The Mexico City Tourist Office, Mexican Ministry of Tourism (Sectur), and the Hotel Association have stands in the arrival areas that can provide information and find you a room for the night.

If you're taking a taxi, purchase your ticket at one of the official airport taxi counters marked Transportación Terrestre (ground transportation), located in the baggage-carousel areas as well as in the concourse area and curbside. Government-controlled fares are based on which colonia you are going to and are usually about $7 (per car, not per person) to most hotels. A 10% tip is customary for airport drivers if they help with baggage.

➤ Airport Information: **Mexico City** (Aeropuerto Internacional Benito Juárez, ☎ 5/571–3600).

Bus Travel

Getting to Mexico by bus is no longer for just the adventurous or budget-conscious. Gateway cities in Texas, along with Tijuana, are served by several small private bus lines as well as by Greyhound. In Mexico, platform announcements are in Spanish only.

Within the city, the Mexico City bus system is used by millions of commuters because it's cheap and goes everywhere. One of the principal bus routes runs along Paseo de la Reforma, Avenida Juárez, and Calle Madero. This west–east route connects Bosque de Chapultepec with the Zócalo. A southbound bus may be taken along Avenida Insurgentes Sur to San Angel and University City, or northbound along Avenida Insurgentes Norte to the Guadalupe Basilica. Mexico City Tourism offices provide free bus-route maps. The price was raised at the end of 1996 from 1 to a maximum 3.50 pesos (about 35¢), depending on how far you're going.

CLASSES

For travel within Mexico, buses run the gamut from comfortable air-conditioned coaches with bathrooms, video movies, and refreshments to dilapidated "vintage" buses (second and third class) on which pigs and chickens travel and frequent stops are made. Fares for the latter are generally up to 30% cheaper than those in the premium categories. Tickets for first class or better—unlike tickets for the other classes—can and should be reserved in advance. Reserved-seat tickets can be purchased at Mexico City travel agencies. Smoking is prohibited on all first-class and deluxe buses.

Buses depart from four outlying stations (*terminales de autobuses*), where tickets can also be purchased: Central de Autobuses del Norte, going north; Central de Autobuses del Sur, going south; Central de Autobuses del Oriente, going east; and Terminal de Autobuses del Poniente, going west.

➤ **Bus Information: ADO** and **ADO GL** (☎ 5/133–2424, 5/133–2444, 5/785–9659, or 01–800/702–8000). **Cristóbal Colón** (☎ 5/756–9926). **Estrella Blanca** (☎ 5/729–0707). **ETN** (☎ 5/577–6529, 5/271–1262, 5/277–6529, or ☎ 5/273–0251). **Estrella Blanca** (☎ 5/729–0707). **Estrella de Oro** (☎ 5/549–8520). **Greyhound** (☎ 800/231–2222, ⊠ Paseo de la Reforma 35, ☎ 5/592–3766). ➤ **Stations: Central de Autobuses del Norte** (⊠ Av. Cién Metros 4907, ☎ 5/587–1552). **Central de Autobuses del Sur** (⊠ Tasqueña 1320, ☎ 5/689–9745). **Central de Autobuses del Oriente** (⊠ Ignacio Zaragoza 200, ☎ 5/762–5977). **Terminal de Autobuses del Poniente** (⊠ Río Tacubaya and Sur 122, ☎ 5/271–4519).

PESERO TRAVEL

Peseros are minibuses that operate on a number of fixed routes and charge a flat rate (a peso once upon a time, hence the name). Peseros pick up passengers at bus stops and outside almost all metro stations. Just stand on the curb, check the route sign on the oncoming pesero's windshield, and hold out your hand. Tell the driver where to stop, or press the button by the back door. If it's really crowded, just bang on the ceiling and yell, "Baja," ("getting off"). The fare is 2 to 3.50 pesos.

Business Hours

BANKS & OFFICES

Banks are generally open weekdays 9–3. In Mexico City, most are open until 5 or 7. Many of the larger banks keep a few branches open Saturday from 9 or 10 to 2:30 and Sunday 10–1:30; however, the extended hours are often for deposits or check cashing only. Government offices are usually open to the public 8–3; along with banks and most private offices, they're closed on national holidays.

GAS STATIONS

Gas stations in general are open 7 AM–10 PM. Those near major thoroughfares in big cities stay open 24 hours, including most holidays.

MUSEUMS & SIGHTS

Along with theaters and most archaeological sights, museums are closed on Monday, with few exceptions. Museums across the country have free admission on Sunday. Hours are normally 9–5 or 6.

SHOPS

Stores are generally open weekdays and Saturday from 9 or 10 AM to 7 or 8 PM; in resort areas, shops may also be open on Sunday. In some resort areas and small towns, shops may close for a two-hour lunch break—about 2–4. Airport shops are open for business seven days a week.

Car Rental

When you think about renting a car, bear in mind that you may be sharing the road with bad local drivers—sometimes acquiring a driver's license in Mexico is more a question of paying someone off than of having tested skill.

Rates begin at $65 a day and $445 a week in Mexico City for an economy car with air-conditioning, a manual transmission, and unlimited mileage. This doesn't include tax on car rentals, which is 15%, or insurance, which runs about $100 a week. *See* Insurance *in* Car Travel, *below*. The major companies tend to be more reliable than local car-rental agencies.

➤ MAJOR AGENCIES: **Alamo** (☎ 800/522–9696; 020/8759–6200 in the U.K. ☎). **Avis** (☎ 800/331–1084; 800/331–1084 in Canada; 02/9353–9000 in Australia; 09/525–1982 in New Zealand ☎). **Budget** (☎ 800/527–0700; 0870/607–5000 in the U.K., through affiliate Europcar ☎). **Dollar** (☎ 800/800–6000; 0124/622–0111 in the U.K., through affiliate Sixt Kenning; 02/9223–1444 in Australia ☎). **Hertz** (☎ 800/654–3001; 800/263–0600 in Canada; 020/8897–2072 in the U.K.; 02/9669–2444 in Australia; 09/256–8690 in New Zealand ☎). **National Car Rental** (☎ 800/227–7368; 020/8680–4800 in the U.K., where it is known as National Europe ☎).

INSURANCE

When driving a rented car you are generally responsible for any damage to or loss of the vehicle as well as for any property damage or personal injury that you may cause. Before you rent, see what coverage your personal auto-insurance policy and credit cards already provide. In Mexico you must have Mexican auto insurance (☞ Car Travel, *below*).

REQUIREMENTS & RESTRICTIONS

In Mexico your own driver's license is acceptable. An International Driver's Permit is a good idea; it's available from the U.S. and Canadian automobile associations, and, in the United Kingdom, from the Automobile Association or Royal Automobile Club. These international permits are universally recognized, and having one in your wallet may save you a problem with the local authorities.

Car Travel

Millions of intrepid drivers brave Mexico City's streets every day and survive, but for out-of-towners the experience can be frazzling. One-way streets are confusing, rush-hour traffic is nightmarish, and parking places can be hard to come by. Police tow trucks haul away illegally parked vehicles, and the owner is heavily fined. As in any large city, getting your car back here is a byzantine process. Locatel (☎ 5/658–1111) is an efficient 24-hour service for tracing vehicles that are towed, stolen, or lost (in case you forgot where you parked). There's a chance an operator on duty may speak English, but the service is primarily in Spanish.

Also keep in mind that the strictly enforced law *Hoy No Circula* (Today My Car Can't Circulate) applies to all private vehicles. One of several efforts to reduce smog and traffic congestion, this law prohibits vehicles from being used on one designated weekday. During emergency smog-alerts, usually in December and January, cars are prohibited from circulating on two days of the week. Cars in violation are impounded by the police. Expect a hefty fine as well.

The weekday you can't drive is specified by the last number or letter of the license plate: on a non-emergency week, 5–6 are prohibited on Monday; 7–8 on Tuesday; 3–4 on Wednesday; 1–2 on Thursday; and 9–0 on Friday. For further information, contact the Mexican Government Tourism Office nearest you.

There are two absolutely essential points to remember about driving in Mexico. First and foremost is to **carry Mexican auto insurance.** (☞ Insurance, *below.*)

Point No. 2: **if you enter Mexico with a car, you must leave with it.** In recent years, the high rate of U.S. vehicles being sold illegally in Mexico has caused the Mexican government to enact stringent regulations for bringing a car into the country. In order to drive into the country, **you must cross the border with the following documents:** title or registration for your vehicle; a birth certificate or passport; a credit card (AE, DC, MC, or V); a valid driver's license with a photo. The title holder, driver, and credit-card owner must be one and the same. For financed, leased, rental, or company cars, **you must bring a notarized letter of permission** from the bank, lien holder, rental agency, or company.

When you submit your paperwork at the border and pay a $12 charge on your credit card, you'll receive a tourist visa, a car permit, and a sticker to put on your vehicle, all valid for up to six months. **Be sure to turn in the permit and the sticker** at the border prior to their expiration date; otherwise you could incur high fines.

One alternative is to **have your paperwork done in advance** at a branch of Sanborn's Mexican Insurance; look in the Yellow Pages for an office in almost every town on the U.S.–Mexico border. You'll still have to go through some of the procedures at the border, but all your paperwork will be in order, and

Sanborn's express window will ensure that you get through relatively quickly. There is a $10 charge for this service. The fact that you drove in with a car is stamped on your tourist card, which you must give to immigration authorities at departure. If an emergency arises and you must fly home, there are complicated customs procedures to face.

EMERGENCY SERVICES

To help motorists on major highways, the Mexican Tourism Ministry operates a fleet of more than 350 pickup trucks, known as the Angeles Verdes, or Green Angels. The bilingual drivers provide mechanical help, first aid, radio-telephone communication, basic supplies and small parts, towing, tourist information, and protection. Services are free, and spare parts, fuel, and lubricants are provided at cost. Tips are always appreciated (figure $5–$10 for big jobs, $2–$3 for minor repairs). The Green Angels patrol fixed sections of the major highways twice daily 8–8 (later on holiday weekends).

➤ CONTACTS: **Green Angels**, Mexico City (☎ 5/250–8221).

INSURANCE

You must **carry Mexican auto insurance**, which you can purchase near border crossings on either the U.S. or Mexican side. If you injure anyone in an accident, you could well be jailed—whether it was your fault or not—unless you have insurance.

➤ CONTACTS: **Instant Mexico Auto Insurance** (✉ 223 Via de San Ysidro, San Ysidro, CA 92173, ☎ 619/428–3583). **Oscar Padilla** (✉ 4330 La Jolla Village Dr., San Diego, CA 92122, ☎ 800/258–8600). **Sanborn's Mexican Insurance** (✉ 2009 S. 10th St., McAllen, TX 78503, ☎ 210/686–0711).

ROAD CONDITIONS

There are several well-kept toll roads in Mexico—most of them four lanes wide. However, these *carreteras* (major highways) don't go too far out of the capital into the countryside. (*Cuota* means toll road; *libre* means no toll, and such roads are two lanes and usually not as smooth.) Some excellent new roads have opened in the past seven or so years, making car travel safer and faster. However, tolls as high as $40 one way can make using these thoroughfares prohibitively expensive.

The Mexican Tourism Ministry distributes free road maps from its tourism offices outside the country. Guía Roji and Pemex (the government petroleum monopoly) publish current city, regional, and national road maps, which are available in bookstores and big supermarket chains for under $10; gas stations generally do not carry maps.

RULES OF THE ROAD

When you sign up for Mexican car insurance, you should receive a booklet on Mexican rules of the road. Read this booklet in order to avoid breaking laws that differ from those of your native country.

If an oncoming vehicle flicks its lights at you in daytime, slow down: it could mean trouble ahead. When approaching a narrow bridge, the first vehicle to flash its lights has right of way. One-way streets are common. A circle with a diagonal line superimposed on the letter E (for *estacionamiento*) means "no parking." Other road signs follow the now widespread system of international symbols, a copy of which will usually be provided when you rent a car in Mexico.

SAFETY ON THE ROAD

First of all, **never drive at night** in Mexico. *Banditos* are one concern, but so are potholes, cars with no working lights, road-hogging trucks, and difficulty in getting assistance. It's best to use toll roads whenever possible; although costly, they're much safer.

Some of the biggest hassles on the road might be from police who pull you over for supposedly breaking the law, or for being a good prospect for a scam. Remember to **be polite**—displays of anger will only make matters worse—and be aware that a police officer might be pulling you over for something you didn't do. Corruption is a fact of life in Mexico. If you are stopped for speeding, the officer is supposed to take your license and hold it until you pay the fine at the local police station. But the officer will always prefer a *mordida* (small bribe) to wasting his time at the police station. If you decide to dispute a charge, do so with a smile, and tell the officer that you would like to talk to the police captain when you get to the station. The officer usually will let you go rather than go to the station.

Customs & Duties

When shopping, **keep receipts** for all purchases. Upon reentering the country, **be ready to show customs officials what you've bought.** If you feel a duty is incorrect or object to the way your clearance was handled, note the inspector's badge number and ask to see a supervisor. If the problem isn't resolved, write to the appropriate authorities, beginning with the port director at your point of entry.

IN AUSTRALIA

Australian residents who are 18 or older may bring home A$400 of souvenirs and gifts (including jewelry), 250 cigarettes or 250 grams of tobacco, and 1,125 milliliters of alcohol (including wine, beer, and spirits). Residents under 18 may bring back A$200 in goods. Prohibited items include meat products. Seeds, plants, and fruits need to be declared upon arrival.

➤ INFORMATION: **Australian Customs Service** (Regional Director, ✉ Box 8, Sydney, NSW 2001, ☎ 02/9213–2000, FAX 02/9213–4000).

IN CANADA

Canadian residents who have been out of Canada for at least seven days may bring home C$500 worth of goods duty-free. If you've been away fewer than seven days but more than 48 hours, the duty-free allowance drops to C$200; if your trip lasts

24 to 48 hours, the allowance is C$50. You may not pool allowances with family members. Goods claimed under the C$500 exemption may follow you by mail; those claimed under the lesser exemptions must accompany you. Alcohol and tobacco products may be included in the seven-day and 48-hour exemptions but not in the 24-hour exemption. If you meet the age requirements of the province or territory through which you reenter Canada, you may bring in, duty-free, 1.14 liters (40 imperial ounces) of wine or liquor or 24 12-ounce cans or bottles of beer or ale. If you are 16 or older you may bring in, duty-free, 200 cigarettes and 50 cigars. Check ahead of time with Revenue Canada or the Department of Agriculture for policies regarding meat products, seeds, plants, and fruits.

You may send an unlimited number of gifts worth up to C$60 each duty-free to Canada. Label the package UNSOLICITED GIFT— VALUE UNDER $60. Alcohol and tobacco are excluded.

➤ INFORMATION: **Revenue Canada** (✉ 2265 St. Laurent Blvd. S, Ottawa, Ontario K1G 4K3, ☎ 613/993–0534, 800/461–9999 in Canada, FAX 613/957–8911, www.ccra-adrc.gc.ca).

IN MEXICO
Upon entering Mexico, you'll be given a baggage declaration form and asked to itemize what you're bringing into the country. You are allowed to bring in 2 liters of spirits or wine for personal use; 400 cigarettes, 50 cigars, or 250 grams of tobacco; a reasonable amount of perfume for personal use; one movie camera and one regular camera and 12 rolls of film for each; and gift items not to exceed a total of $300. If driving across the U.S. border, gift items must not exceed $50. You aren't allowed to bring firearms, meat, vegetables, plants, fruit, or flowers into the country.

IN NEW ZEALAND
Homeward-bound residents 17 or older may bring back NZ$700 worth of souvenirs and gifts. Your duty-free allowance also

includes 4.5 liters of wine or beer; one 1,125-milliliter bottle of spirits; and either 200 cigarettes, 250 grams of tobacco, 50 cigars, or a combination of the three up to 250 grams. Prohibited items include meat products, seeds, plants, and fruits.

➤ **INFORMATION: New Zealand Customs** (Custom House, ⊠ 50 Anzac Ave., Box 29, Auckland, New Zealand, ☎ 09/359–6655, FAX 09/359–6732).

IN THE U.K.

From countries outside the EU, including Mexico, you may bring home, duty-free, 200 cigarettes or 50 cigars; 1 liter of spirits or 2 liters of fortified or sparkling wine or liqueurs; 2 liters of still table wine; 60 milliliters of perfume; 250 milliliters of toilet water; plus £136 of other goods, including gifts and souvenirs. Prohibited items include meat products, seeds, plants, and fruits.

➤ **INFORMATION: HM Customs and Excise** (⊠ Dorset House, Stamford St., Bromley, Kent BR1 1XX, ☎ 020/7202–4227).

IN THE U.S.

U.S. residents who have been out of the country for at least 48 hours (and who have not used the $400 allowance or any part of it in the past 30 days) may bring home $400 worth of foreign goods duty-free.

U.S. residents 21 and older may bring back 1 liter of alcohol duty-free. In addition, regardless of your age, you are allowed 200 cigarettes and 100 non-Cuban cigars. Antiques, which the U.S. Customs Service defines as objects more than 100 years old, enter duty-free, as do original artworks done entirely by hand, including paintings, drawings, and sculptures.

You may also send packages home duty-free: up to $200 worth of goods for personal use, with a limit of one parcel per addressee per day (except alcohol or tobacco products or perfume worth more than $5); label the package PERSONAL USE and attach a list of its contents and their retail value. Do not label the package UNSOLICITED GIFT or your duty-free exemption will drop to $100. Mailed items do not affect your duty-free allowance on your return.

➤ INFORMATION: **U.S. Customs Service** (✉ 1300 Pennsylvania Ave. NW, Washington, DC 20229, www.customs.gov; inquiries ☎ 202/354–1000; complaints c/o ✉ Office of Regulations and Rulings; registration of equipment c/o ✉ Resource Management, ☎ 202/927–0540).

Electricity

For U.S. and Canadian travelers, electrical converters are not necessary because Mexico operates on the 60-cycle, 120-volt system; however, many Mexican outlets have not been updated to accommodate three-prong and polarized plugs (those with one larger prong), so to be safe **bring an adapter.**

If your appliances are dual-voltage you'll need only an adapter. Don't use 110-volt outlets, marked FOR SHAVERS ONLY, for high-wattage appliances such as blow-dryers. Most laptops operate equally well on 110 and 220 volts and so require only an adapter.

Embassies

If you need assistance in an emergency, you can go to your country's embassy. Proof of identity and citizenship are generally required to enter.

The U.S. Embassy is open weekdays 9–2 and 3–5, but is closed for American and Mexican holidays; however, there's always a duty officer to take emergency calls on holidays and after closing hours. The embassy keeps a list of English-speaking local doctors on hand if you need to consult one. The Canadian Embassy is open weekdays 9–1 and 2–5 and is closed for Canadian and Mexican holidays. The British Embassy is open weekdays 8:30–3:30.

➤ AUSTRALIA: **Australian Embassy** ✉ Rubén Darío 55, Col. Polanco, ☎ 5/531–5225.

➤ **Canada: Canadian Embassy** ⊠ Schiller 529, Col. Polanco, ☎ 5/724–7900.

➤ **New Zealand: New Zealand Embassy** ⊠ José Luis LaGrange 103, 10th fl., Col. Polanco, ☎ 5/281–5486.

➤ **United Kingdom: British Embassy** ⊠ Río Lerma 71, ☎ 5/207–2449.

➤ **United States: U.S. Embassy** (⊠ Paseo de la Reforma 305, Col. Cuauhtémoc, ☎ 5/209–9100).

Emergencies

You're not protected by the laws of your native land once you're on Mexican soil. If you get into a scrape with the law, you can call the Citizens' Emergency Center in the United States. You can also call the 24-hour English-language hot line of the Procuraduría de Protecciónal Turista (Attorney General for the Protection of Tourists) in Mexico City; it can provide immediate assistance as well as general, nonemergency guidance. **In an emergency, dial 07 from any phone.**

➤ **Contacts: Citizens' Emergency Center**(☎ 202/647–5225 weekdays 8:15 AM–10 PM EST, Sat. 9AM–3 PM; ☎ 202/634–3600 after hours andSun.). **Procuraduría de Protección al Turista** (Attorney General for the Protection of Tourists; ☎ 01–800/903–9200, 800/482–9832 from the U.S.).

Etiquette & Behavior

In the United States, being direct, efficient, and succinct is highly valued. But in Mexico, where communication tends to be more subtle, this style is often perceived as rude and aggressive. Mexicans are extremely polite. **Remember that things move at a slow pace** here and that there's no stigma attached to being late. Learning basic phrases in Spanish such as "please" and "thank you" will make a big difference in how people respond to you.

BUSINESS ETIQUETTE

Personal relationships always come first here, so developing rapport and trust is essential. A handshake and personal greeting is appropriate along with a friendly inquiry about family, especially if you have met the family. In established business relationships, don't be surprised if you are greeted with a kiss on the check or a hug. Always be respectful toward colleagues in public and keep confrontations private. Meetings may or may not start on time, but you should be patient. When invited to dinner at the home of a client or associate, bring a gift and be sure to send a thank-you note afterward.

Health

AIR POLLUTION

Air pollution in Mexico City can pose a health risk. Children, the elderly, and those with respiratory problems are advised to avoid jogging, participating in outdoor sports, and being outdoors more than necessary on days of high smog alerts. If you have heart problems, keep in mind that Mexico City is, at 7,556 feet, the highest metropolis in North America. This compounded with the smog may pose a serious health risk, so check with your doctor before planning a trip.

The Australian, British, Canadian, New Zealand, and U.S. embassies in Mexico City can provide lists of English-speaking doctors.

FOOD & DRINK

In Mexico the major health risk, known as *turista*, or traveler's diarrhea, is caused by eating contaminated fruit or vegetables or drinking contaminated water. Stay away from ice, uncooked food, and unpasteurized milk and milk products, and **drink only bottled water** or water that has been boiled for at least 10 minutes (*quiero el agua hervida por diez minutos*), even when you're brushing your teeth. Mild cases may respond to Imodium (known generically as loperamide or Lomotil) or Pepto-Bismol (not as strong), both of which can be purchased over the counter. Drink plenty of purified water or tea; chamomile tea (*te de manzanilla*) is a good folk remedy and it's readily available in restaurants throughout Mexico. In severe cases, rehydrate yourself with Gatorade or a salt–sugar solution (¼ teaspoon salt and 4 tablespoons sugar per quart of water).

When ordering cold drinks at untouristed establishments, **skip the ice:** *sin hielo.* (You can usually identify ice made commercially from purified water by its uniform shape and the hole in the center.) Hotels with water-purification systems will post signs to that effect in the rooms. *Tacos al pastor*—thin pork slices grilled on a spit and garnished with cilantro, onions, and chili peppers—are delicious but dangerous. It's also a good idea to pass up *ceviche*, raw fish cured in lemon juice—a favorite appetizer, especially at seaside resorts. Marinating in lemon juice does not constitute the "cooking" that would make the shellfish safe to eat. Also, be wary of hamburgers sold from street stands: horse meat is common.

MEDICAL PLANS

No one plans to get sick while traveling, but it happens, so **consider signing up with a medical-assistance company.** Members get doctor referrals, emergency evacuation or repatriation, hot lines for medical consultation, cash for emergencies, and other assistance.

➤ MEDICAL-ASSISTANCE COMPANIES: **International SOS Assistance** (✉ 8 Neshaminy Interplex, Suite 207, Trevose, PA 19053, ☎ 215/245–4707, 800/523–6586, FAX 215/244–9617; ✉ 12 Chemin Riantbosson, 1217 Meyrin 1, Geneva, Switzerland, ☎ 4122/785–6464, FAX 4122/785–6424; ✉ 331 N. Bridge Rd., 17-00, Odeon Towers, Singapore 188720, ☎ 65/338–7800, FAX 65/338–7611; www.internationalsos.com).

SHOTS & MEDICATIONS

According to the U.S. National Centers for Disease Control and Prevention (CDC), there is a limited risk of malaria and dengue fever in certain rural areas of Mexico. In most urban or easily accessible areas you need not worry. However, if you plan to visit remote regions or stay for more than six weeks, **check with the CDC's International Travelers Hotline.** In areas where malaria and dengue, both of which are carried by mosquitoes, are prevalent, use mosquito nets, wear clothing that covers the body, apply repellent containing DEET, and use spray for flying insects in living and sleeping areas. Repellents (*repelentes contra moscas*) and sprays (*repelentes de sprie contra moscas*) can be purchased at pharmacies.

➤ HEALTH WARNINGS: **National Centers for Disease Control and Prevention** (CDC; National Center for Infectious Diseases, Division of Quarantine, Traveler's Health Section, ✉ 1600 Clifton Rd. NE, M/S E-03, Atlanta, GA 30333, ☎ 888/232–3228, FAX 888/232–3299, www.cdc.gov).

➤ HOSPITAL: **American British Cowdray Hospital** (✉ Calle Sur 136–116, corner of Observatorio, Col. las Américas, ☎ 5/230–8161 for emergencies, 5/230–8000 switchboard).

Holidays & Festivals

Mexico is the land of festivals; if you reserve lodging well in advance, they're a golden opportunity to have a thoroughly Mexican experience. January is full of long, regional festivals.

Banks and government offices close during Holy Week (the week leading to Easter Sunday) and on Cinco de Mayo, Día de la Raza, and Day of the Dead. Government offices usually have reduced hours and staff from Christmas through New Year's Day.

Language

Spanish is the official language of Mexico, although Indian languages are spoken by approximately 20% of the population and those people speak no Spanish at all. Basic English is widely understood by most people employed in tourism. At the very least, shopkeepers will know the numbers for bargaining purposes.

As in most other foreign countries, knowing the mother tongue has a way of opening doors, so **learn some Spanish words and phrases.** Mexicans welcome even the most halting attempts to use the language.

Money Matters

Prices in this book are quoted most often in U.S. dollars. We would prefer to list costs in pesos, but because the value of the currency fluctuates considerably, what costs 90 pesos today might cost 120 pesos in six months.

Mexico is inexpensive, compared to other North American vacation spots. The devaluation of the peso, started in late 1994, has made this especially true, though prices of the large chain hotels, calculated in dollars, have not gone down, and some restaurant owners and merchants have raised their prices to compensate for the devaluation. In general, costs will vary with when, where, and how you travel in Mexico. If you want a closer look at the country and are not wedded to standard creature comforts, you can spend as little as $25 a day on room, board, and local transportation.

Mexico City is, however, one of the more expensive places to visit in the country. A stay in one of the city's top hotels can cost more than $200 (as much or more than at the coastal resorts), but you can get away with a tab of $45 for two at what was once an expensive restaurant.

ATMS

ATMs (*caja automática*) are becoming commonplace in more and more Mexican towns and cities. Cirrus and Plus are the most commonly found networks in Mexico. Before you leave home, ask what the transaction fee will be for withdrawing money in Mexico. (It's usually $3 a pop.) Many Mexican ATMs cannot accept PINs (personal identification numbers) that have more than four digits; if yours is longer, ask your bank about changing your PIN (*numero de clave*) before you leave home, and keep in mind that processing such a change often takes a few weeks.

For cash advances, plan to use Visa or MasterCard, as many Mexican ATMs don't accept American Express. The ATMs at Banamex, one of the oldest nationwide banks, tend to be the most reliable. Bancomer is another bank with many ATM locations, but they usually provide only cash advances. The newer Serfín banks have reliable ATMs that accept credit cards as well as Plus and Cirrus cards.

CREDIT CARDS

Traveler's checks and all major U.S. credit cards are accepted in most of Mexico City. Smaller, less expensive restaurants and shops, however, tend to take only cash. The most widely accepted cards are Mastercard and Visa. When shopping, you can usually get better prices if you pay with cash.

At the same time, when traveling internationally you will receive wholesale exchange rates when you make purchases with credit cards. These exchange rates are usually better than rates that banks give you for changing money. In Mexico the decision to pay cash or use a credit card might depend on whether the establishment in which you are making a purchase finds bargaining for prices acceptable. To avoid fraud, it's wise to make sure that "pesos" is clearly marked on all credit-card receipts.

Throughout this guide, the following abbreviations are used: **AE**, American Express; **DC**, Diner's Club; **MC**, MasterCard; and **V**, Visa.

➤ REPORTING LOST CARDS: Before you leave for Mexico, be sure to find out your credit-card companies' toll-free card-

replacement numbers that work at home as well as in Mexico; they could be impossible to find once you get to Mexico, and the calls you place to cancel your cards can be long ones. **Carry these numbers separately from your wallet** so you'll have them if you need to call to report lost or stolen cards.

CURRENCY

At press time, the peso was still "floating" after the devaluation enacted by the Zedillo administration in late 1994. While exchange rates have been as favorable as 9.85 pesos to US$1, 6.40 pesos to C$1, 15.40 pesos to £1, 6.10 pesos to A$1, and 4.85 pesos to NZ$1, the market and prices continue to adjust. **Check with your bank or the financial pages of your local newspaper for current exchange rates.** For quick estimates of how much something costs in U.S. dollar terms, divide prices given in pesos by 10. For example, 50 pesos would be about $5.

Mexican currency comes in denominations of 10-, 20-, 50-, 100-, 200-, 500-, and 1,000-peso bills. Coins come in denominations of 20, 10, and 5 pesos and 50, 20, 10, and 5 centavos. Many of the coins and bills are very similar, so check carefully.

CURRENCY EXCHANGE

ATM transaction fees may be higher abroad than at home, but ATM currency-exchange rates are the best of all because they're based on wholesale rates offered only by major banks.

Most banks change money on weekdays only until 1 (though they stay open until 5), while casas de cambio generally stay open until 6 and often operate on weekends. Bank rates are regulated by the federal government and are therefore invariable, while casas de cambio have slightly more variable rates. Some hotels also exchange money, but for providing you with this convenience they help themselves to a bigger commission than banks.

When changing money, count your bills before leaving the bank or casa de cambio, and don't accept any partially torn or taped-together notes; they won't be accepted anywhere. Also, many shop and restaurant owners are unable to make change for large bills. Request *billetes chicos* (small bills) when you exchange money.

➤ EXCHANGE SERVICES: **International Currency Express** (☎ 888/278–6628 for orders, www.foreignmoney.com). **Thomas Cook Currency Services** (☎ 800/287–7362, www.us.thomascook.com).

TRAVELER'S CHECKS

Lost or stolen traveler's checks can usually be replaced within 24 hours. To ensure a speedy refund, buy your own traveler's checks—don't let someone else pay for them: irregularities like this can cause delays. The person who bought the checks should make the call to request a refund.

Passports & Visas

When traveling internationally, **carry your passport even if you don't need one** (it's always the best form of I.D.) and **make two photocopies of the data page** (one for someone at home and another for you, carried separately from your passport). If you lose your passport, promptly call the nearest embassy or consulate and the local police.

ENTERING MEXICO

For stays of up to 180 days, Americans must prove citizenship through either a valid passport, certified copy of a birth certificate, or voter-registration card (the last two must be accompanied by a government-issue photo ID). All children, including infants, must have proof of citizenship for travel to Mexico. Children up to age 18 traveling with a single parent must also have a notarized letter from the other parent stating that the child has his or her permission to leave their home country. If the other parent is deceased or the child has only one legal parent, a notarized statement saying so must be obtained as proof. For stays of more than 180 days, all U.S. citizens, even infants, need a valid passport to enter Mexico. Minors also need parental permission.

Canadians need only proof of citizenship to enter Mexico for stays of up to six months.

U.K. citizens need only a valid passport to enter Mexico for stays of up to three months.

Mexico has instituted a $15 visitor fee that applies to all visitors except those entering by sea at Mexican ports who stay less than 72 hours and those entering by land who do not stray past the 26–30-km (16–18-mi) checkpoint into the country's interior. For visitors arriving by air, the fee, which covers visits of more than 72 hours and up to 30 days, is usually tacked on to the airline-ticket price. You must pay the fee each time you extend your 30-day tourist visa.

PASSPORT OFFICES

The best time to apply for a passport or to renew is in fall and winter. Before any trip, check your passport's expiration date, and, if necessary, renew it as soon as possible.

➤ **AUSTRALIAN CITIZENS: Australian Passport Office** (☎ 131–232, www.dfat.gov.au/passports).

➤ **CANADIAN CITIZENS: Passport Office** (☎ 819/994–3500, 800/567–6868, www.dfait-maeci.gc.ca/passport).

➤ **NEW ZEALAND CITIZENS: New Zealand Passport Office** (☎ 04/494–0700, www.passports.govt.nz).

➤ **U.K. CITIZENS: London Passport Office** (☎ 0990/210–410), for fees and documentation requirements and to request an emergency passport.

➤ **U.S. CITIZENS: National Passport Information Center** (☎ 900/225–5674; calls are 35¢ per minute for automated service, $1.05 per minute for operator service).

Safety

The U.S. State Department has warned of "critical levels" of crime against tourists in Mexico, noting an increase in the level of violence of the crimes committed and what appeared to be a significant incidence of sexual assaults against women. Reports indicated that uniformed police officers were on occasion perpetrating the nonviolent crimes, sometimes stopping cars and seeking money (☞ Safety on the Road in Car Travel, *above*).

The largest increase in crime has taken place in Mexico City, where the age-old problem of pickpocketing has been overshadowed by robberies at gunpoint. Another development has been abductions and robberies in taxicabs hailed from the street (as opposed to hired from a hotel or taxi stand).

Many foreigners are aware of Mexico's reputation for corruption. Everyone has heard some horror story about highway assaults, pickpocketing, bribes, or foreigners languishing in Mexican jails. These reports of crimes apply in large part to Mexico City (and more remote areas of Oaxaca and Chiapas). Don't pick up hitchhikers or hitchhike yourself. Also, try to use luxury buses (rather than second- or third-class vehicles), which use the safer toll roads—and it's best to travel only during the day. Don't venture alone onto uncrowded beaches, and everyone should **avoid urges to get away from it all** on your own (even as a couple) to go hiking in remote national parks.

Don't wear any valuables, including watches. Wear a money belt, put valuables in hotel safes, and carry your own baggage whenever possible, unless in a luxury hotel. Also, you won't need your passport in the city, so leave it in the hotel safe. **Do not hail taxis on the street under any circumstances.** If you must use an ATM, do so during the day and in big, enclosed commercial areas. Avoid the glass-enclosed street variety of banks where you may be more vulnerable to thieves who force you to withdraw money for them; abduction is also possible.

Bear in mind that reporting a crime to the police is often a frustrating experience unless you speak excellent Spanish and have a great deal of patience. If you are the victim of an assault, contact your local consular agent or the consular section of your country's embassy in Mexico City, especially if you need medical attention.

WOMEN IN MEXICO

Women traveling alone are likely to be subjected to *piropos* (catcalls). To avoid this, don't wear tight or provocative clothes or enter street bars or cantinas alone. Your best strategy is always to ignore the offender, do not speak to him, and go on about your business. If the situation seems to be getting out of hand, don't hesitate to ask someone for help. Piropos are one thing, but more serious harassment of women is not considered acceptable behavior in Mexico. If you express outrage, you should find no shortage of willing defenders.

Subway Travel

Transporting 5 million passengers daily, Mexico City's metro is one of the world's best, busiest, safest, and cheapest transportation systems—1.50 pesos (about 15¢). Many stations have temporary cultural displays ranging from archaeological treasures to modern art; the Pino Suárez station has a small Aztec pyramid inside, a surprise discovery during construction.

There are 10 intersecting metro lines covering more than 160 km (100 mi). User-friendly, color-coded maps are sometimes available free at metro-station information desks (if there's an attendant) and at Mexico City tourism offices; color-keyed signs and maps are posted all around. Hours vary somewhat according to the line, but service is essentially 5 AM–midnight weekdays; 6 AM–2 AM Saturday; 6 AM–1 AM Sunday and holidays.

Taxes

Mexico charges an airport departure tax of US$18 or the peso equivalent for international and domestic flights. This tax is usually included in the price of your ticket, but check to be certain. Traveler's checks and credit cards are not accepted at the airport as payment for this.

VALUE-ADDED TAX

Mexico has a value-added tax of 15%, called I.V.A. (*impuesto de valor agregado*), which is occasionally (and illegally) waived for cash purchases. Other taxes and charges apply for phone calls made from your hotel room.

Taxis

The Mexico City variety comes in several colors, types, and sizes. Unmarked, or *turismo*, sedans with hooded meters are usually stationed outside major hotels and in tourist areas; however, they are uneconomical for short trips. Their drivers are almost always English-speaking guides and can be hired for sightseeing on a daily or hourly basis. Always negotiate the price in advance; many drivers will start by asking how much you want to pay to get a sense of how street-smart you are. Sitio taxis operate out of stands, take radio calls, and are authorized to charge a small premium. Among these, Servi-Taxis and Taxi-Mex, which accepts American Express, offer 24-hour service.

Government-certified taxis have a license with a photo of the driver and a taxi number prominently displayed, a meter, and either an orange or green stripe at the bottom of the license plate. In many cities, taxis charge by zones. **Hire taxis only from hotels and sitios, or use those that you have summoned by phone.** Street taxis might be the cheapest, but an alarming increase in abductions and violent crime involves street cabs— for safety's sake, don't take one. And never leave luggage unattended in a taxi.

Always **establish the fare beforehand,** and **count your change.**
Be certain that the meter runs before getting in, and remember
that taxi drivers are authorized to charge 10% more at night,
usually after 10. Taking a taxi in Mexico City is extremely
inexpensive and tips are not expected unless you have
luggage—then 10% is sufficient.

➤ TAXI COMPANIES: **Servi-Taxis** (☎ 5/271–2560). **Taxi-Mex** (☎ 5/
538–0912, 5/538–0573).

Telephones

Thanks to its 1991 privatization, Teléfonos de México (Mexico's
phone service) is gradually being overhauled. With the
increased installation of new phone and fax lines in major
Mexican cities, many phone numbers are in the process of being
changed. A recording may offer the new number; learn the
Spanish words for numbers 1 through 9.

AREA & COUNTRY CODES

The country code for Mexico is 52. When calling a Mexico
number from abroad, dial the country code and then all of the
numbers listed for the entry.

DIRECTORY & OPERATOR ASSISTANCE

Directory assistance is 040 nationwide. For international
assistance, dial 00 first for an international operator and most
likely you'll get one that speaks English.

INTERNATIONAL CALLS

To make a call to the United States or Canada, **dial 001 before
the area code and number;** to call Europe, Latin America, or
Japan, **dial 00** before the country and city codes. When calling
home, the country code for the U.S. and Canada is 1, the U.K. 44,
Australia 61, New Zealand 64, and South Africa 27.

LOCAL AND LONG-DISTANCE CALLS

The number of digits you need to dial for local calls varies.
Numbers preceding the "/" in our listings are the area or city

codes, to be dialed when calling long distance within Mexico. However, in Mexico City even when calling locally you now must dial the area code as well as the regular number.

For local or long-distance calls, one option is to find a **caseta de larga distancia,** a telephone service usually operated out of a store such as a *papelería* (stationery store), restaurant, or other small business; look for the phone symbol on the door. Casetas may cost more to use than pay phones, but you have a better chance of immediate success. To make a direct long-distance call, tell the person on duty the number you'd like to call, and he or she will give you a rate and dial for you. It's usually better to call *por cobrar* (collect) from a pay phone.

LONG-DISTANCE SERVICES

AT&T, MCI, and Sprint access codes make calling long distance relatively convenient, but you may find the local access number blocked in many hotel rooms. First ask the hotel operator to connect you. If the hotel operator balks, ask for an international operator, or dial the international operator yourself. One way to improve your odds of getting connected to your long-distance carrier is to travel with more than one company's calling card (a hotel may block Sprint, for example, but not MCI). If all else fails, call from a pay phone.

➤ ACCESS CODES: **AT&T Direct** (☎ 01–800/462–4240). **MCI WorldPhone** (☎ 01–800/674–7000). **Sprint International Access** (☎ 01–800/877–8000).

PHONE CARDS

In most parts of the country now, pay phones accept prepaid cards, called Ladatel cards, sold in 30-, 50- or 100-peso denominations (approximately $3, $5, and $10, respectively) at newsstands or pharmacies. Many pay phones in Mexico only accept these cards; coin-only pay phones are usually broken. Still other phones have two unmarked slots, one for a Ladatel (a Spanish acronym for "long-distance direct dialing") card and the other for a credit card. These are primarily for Mexican bank cards, but some accept Visa or MasterCard, though *not* U.S. telephone credit cards.

To use a Ladatel card, simply insert it in the appropriate slot, dial 001 (for calls to the States) or 01 (for calls in Mexico), and the area code and number you're trying to reach. Credit is deleted from the card as you use it, and your balance is displayed on a small screen on the phone.

TOLL-FREE NUMBERS

Toll-free numbers in Mexico start with an 800 prefix. To reach them, you need to dial 01 before the number. In this guide, Mexico-only toll-free numbers appear as follows: 01–800/12–345 (numbers can also have six or seven digits). Most of the 800 numbers in the book work in the U.S. only and are listed simply: 800/123–4567. Toll-free numbers that work in Canada are labeled accordingly, as are those that work in more than one country.

Time

Mexico has three time zones; most of the country falls in Central Standard Time, which includes Mexico City and is in line with Chicago.

Tipping

When tipping in Mexico, remember that the minimum wage is the equivalent of $3 a day and that the vast majority of workers in the tourist industry live barely above the poverty line. However, there are Mexicans who think in dollars and know, for example, that in the United States porters are tipped about $2 a bag. They may complain either verbally or with a facial expression if they feel they deserve more—you and your conscience must decide.

Tours & Packages

Because everything is prearranged on a prepackaged tour or independent vacation, you'll spend less time planning—and often get it all at a good price.

BOOKING WITH AN AGENT

Travel agents are excellent resources. But it's a good idea to collect brochures from several agencies as some agents' suggestions may be influenced by relationships with tour and package firms that reward them for volume sales. If you have a special interest, **find an agent with expertise in that area**; ASTA (☞ Travel Agencies, *below*) has a database of specialists worldwide.

BUYER BEWARE

Each year consumers are stranded or lose their money when tour operators—even large ones with excellent reputations—go out of business. So **check out the operator.** Ask several travel agents about its reputation, and try to **book with a company that has a consumer-protection program.** In the United States, members of the National Tour Association and the United States Tour Operators Association are required to set aside funds to cover your payments and travel arrangements in the event that the company defaults. It's also a good idea to choose a company that participates in the American Society of Travel Agents' Tour Operator Program (TOP); ASTA will act as mediator in any disputes between you and your tour operator.

➤ TOUR-OPERATOR RECOMMENDATIONS: **American Society of Travel Agents** (☞ Travel Agencies, *below*). **National Tour Association** (NTA; ✉ 546 E. Main St., Lexington, KY 40508, ☎ 606/226-4444, 800/682–8886, www.ntaonline.com). **United States Tour Operators Association** (USTOA; ✉ 342 Madison Ave., Suite 1522, New York, NY 10173, ☎ 212/599–6599, 800/468–7862, FAX 212/599–6744, ustoaaol.com, www.ustoa.com).

156

Train Travel

At press time, only four lines were running between fairly obscure Mexican towns. We don't recommend train travel at this time, but if you're determined to go by rail, you can get information from English-speaking operators about schedules and prices from Ferrocarriles Nacionales de Mexico (National Mexican Railways; ☎ 5/547–1084) in Mexico City.

➤ TRAIN INFORMATION: From the United States, you can get some information on trains and rail-hotel packages by contacting **Mexico by Train** (☎ FAX 956/725–3659, ☎ 800/321–1699).

Travel Agencies

A good travel agent puts your needs first. Look for an agency that has been in business at least five years, emphasizes customer service, and has someone on staff who specializes in your destination. In addition, **make sure the agency belongs to a professional trade organization.** The American Society of Travel Agents, with 27,000 agents in some 170 countries, is the largest and most influential in the field. Operating under the motto "Integrity in Travel," it maintains and enforces a strict code of ethics and will step in to help mediate any agent-client disputes if necessary. ASTA also maintains a Web site that includes a directory of agents. (If a travel agency is also acting as your tour operator, *see* Buyer Beware in Tours & Packages, *above*.)

➤ TRAVEL AGENCIES: **Gray Line Tours** (⊠ Londres 166, ☎ 5/208–1163), **American Express** (⊠ Paseo de la Reforma 234, ☎ 5/326–2831), and **Mexico Travel Advisors** (MTA; ⊠ Génova 30, ☎ 5/525–7520, 5/525–7534).

➤ LOCAL AGENT REFERRALS: **American Society of Travel Agents** (ASTA; ☎ 800/965–2782 24-hr hot line, FAX 703/684–8319, www.astanet.com). **Association of British Travel Agents** (⊠ 68–71 Newman St., London W1P 4AH, ☎ 020/7637–2444, FAX 0171/637–0713, abta.co.uk, www.abtanet.com). **Association of**

Canadian Travel Agents (✉ 1729 Bank St., Suite 201, Ottawa, Ontario K1V 7Z5, ☎ 613/521–0474, FAX 613/521–0805, acta.ntlsympatico.ca). **Australian Federation of Travel Agents** (✉ Level 3, 309 Pitt St., Sydney 2000, ☎ 02/9264–3299, FAX 02/9264–1085, www.afta.com.au). **Travel Agents' Association of New Zealand** (✉ Box 1888, Wellington 10033, ☎ 04/499–0104, FAX 04/499–0827, taanztiasnet.co.nz).

Visitor Information

The **Mexico City Tourist Office** (Departamento de Turismo del Distrito Federal, or DDF) maintains information booths at both the international and domestic arrival areas at the airport. In town, visit the city's tourism module at Amberes 54, at the corner of Londres in the Zona Rosa. This office also provides information by phone with its Infotur service (☎ 5/525–9380) 9–7 daily. Multilingual operators are available and have access to an extensive data bank.

The **Secretariat of Tourism** (Sectur) operates a 24-hour multilingual hot line (☎ 5/250–0123, 5/250–0493, 5/250–0027, 5/250–0589, 5/250–0151, 5/250–0292, 5/250–0741) that provides information on both Mexico City and the entire country. If lines are busy, keep trying. Outside Mexico City, call toll-free (☎ 01–800/903–9200, 800/482–9832) to reach the Sectur Tourist Information Center at Presidente Masarik 172 (in Colonia Polanco), open weekdays 8–8.

➤ MEXICAN GOVERNMENT TOURIST OFFICES (MGO): **United States**: (☎ 800/446–3942 nationwide. **Canada:** (✉ 1 Place Ville Marie, Suite 1510, Montréal, Québec H3B 2B5, ☎ 514/871–1052, FAX 514/871–3825; ✉ 2 Bloor St. W, Suite 1502, Toronto, Ontario M4W 33E2, ☎ 416/925–0704, FAX 416/925–6061; ✉ 999 W. Hastings St., Suite 1610, Vancouver, British Columbia V6C 2WC, ☎ 604/669–2845, FAX 604/669–3498). **United Kingdom:** (✉ 60

Trafalgar Sq., London WC2N 5DS, ☎ 020/7734–1058, FAX 0171/ 930–9202). **Mexico:** (✉ Presidente Masaryk 172, Mexico, D.F. 11550, ☎ 5/250–0123).

➤ U.S. GOVERNMENT ADVISORIES: **U.S. Department of State** (✉ Overseas Citizens Services Office, Room 4811 N.S., 2201 C St. NW, Washington, DC 20520, ☎ 202/647–5225 for interactive hot line, 301/946–4400 for computer bulletin board, FAX 202/ 647–3000 for interactive hot line); enclose a self-addressed, stamped, business-size envelope.

Web Sites

Do check out the World Wide Web when you're planning. You'll find everything from up-to-date weather forecasts to virtual tours of famous cities. Fodor's Web site, at www.fodors.com, is a great place to start your online travels. For more information on Mexico, visit: www.mexico-travel.com and www.safemexico .com.

When to Go

October through May are generally the driest months; during the peak of the rainy season (June–September), it may rain for a few hours daily. But the sun often shines for the rest of the day, and the reduced off-season rates may well compensate for the reduced sunshine.

From December through the second week after Easter, the Mexican resorts—where the vast majority of tourists go—are the most crowded and therefore the most expensive. This also holds true for July and August, school-vacation months, when Mexican families crowd hotels. To avoid the masses, the highest prices, and the worst rains, **consider visiting Mexico during October, November, April, or May,** just not during the traditional holiday periods.

CLIMATE
In general, the high central plateau on which Mexico City, Guadalajara, and many of the country's colonial cities are located is springlike year-round.

➤ Forecasts: **Weather Channel Connection** (☎ 900/932–8437), 95¢ per minute from a Touch-Tone phone.

MEXICO CITY (CENTRAL MEXICO)

Jan.	70F	21C	May	79F	26C	Sept.	72F	22C
	44	6		54	12		52	11
Feb.	73F	23C	June	77F	25C	Oct.	72F	22C
	45	7		54	12		50	10
Mar.	79F	26C	July	73F	23C	Nov.	72F	22C
	48	9		52	11		46	8
Apr.	81F	27C	Aug.	73F	23C	Dec.	70F	21C
	50	10		54	12		45	7

SPANISH VOCABULARY

Note: Mexican Spanish differs from Castilian Spanish.

WORDS AND PHRASES
Basics

ENGLISH	SPANISH	PRONUNCIATION
Yes/no	Sí/no	see/no
Please	Por favor	pore fah-*vore*
May I?	¿Me permite?	may pair-*mee*-tay
Thank you (very much)	(Muchas) gracias	(*moo*-chas) *grah*-see-as
You're welcome	De nada	day *nah*-dah
Excuse me	Con permiso	con pair-*mee*-so
Pardon me/what did you say?	¿Como?/Mánde?	ko-mo/*mahn*-dey
Could you tell me?	¿Podría decirme?	po-*dree*-ah deh-*seer*-meh
I'm sorry	Lo siento	lo see-*en*-toe
Good morning!	¡Buenos días!	*bway*-nohs *dee*-ahs
Good afternoon!	¡Buenas tardes!	*bway*-nahs *tar*-dess
Good evening!	¡Buenas noches!	*bway*-nahs *no*-chess
Goodbye!	¡Adiós!/¡Hasta luego!	ah-dee-*ohss*/*ah*-stah -*lwe*-go
Mr./Mrs.	Señor/Señora	sen-yor/sen-*yore*-ah
Miss	Señorita	sen-yo-*ree*-tah
Pleased to meet you	Mucho gusto	*moo*-cho *goose*-to
How are you?	¿Cómo está usted?	*ko*-mo es-*tah* oo-*sted*
Very well, thank you.	Muy bien, gracias.	*moo*-ee bee-*en*, grah-see-as
And you?	¿Y usted?	ee oos-*ted*
Hello (on the telephone)	Bueno	*bwen*-oh

Numbers

1	un, uno	oon, *oo*-no
2	dos	dos
3	tres	trace
4	cuatro	*kwah*-tro
5	cinco	*sink*-oh
6	seis	sace
7	siete	see-*et*-ey
8	ocho	o-cho
9	nueve	new-ev-ay
10	diez	dee-*es*
11	once	*own*-sey
12	doce	*doe*-sey
13	trece	*tray*-sey
14	catorce	kah-*tor*-sey
15	quince	*keen*-sey
16	dieciséis	dee-es-ee-*sace*
17	diecisiete	dee-es-ee-see-*et*-ay
18	dieciocho	dee-es-ee-o-cho
19	diecinueve	*dee*-es-ee-new-ev-ay
20	veinte	*bain*-tay
21	veinte y uno/veintiuno	*bain*-te-oo-no
30	treinta	*train*-tah
32	treinta y dos	train-tay-*dose*
40	cuarenta	kwah-*ren*-tah
43	cuarenta y tres	kwah-*ren*-tay-*trace*
50	cincuenta	seen-*kwen*-tah
54	cincuenta y cuatro *kwah*-tro	seen-*kwen*-tay
60	sesenta	sess-*en*-tah
65	sesenta y cinco	sess-*en*-tay *seen*-ko
70	setenta	set-*en*-tah
76	setenta y seis	set-*en*-tay *sace*
80	ochenta	oh-*chen*-tah

87	ochenta y siete	oh-*chen*-tay *see*-*yet*-ay
90	noventa	no-*ven*-tah
98	noventa y ocho	no-*ven*-tah *o*-cho
100	cien	*see*-en
101	ciento uno	see-en-toe *oo*-no
200	doscientos	doe-see-*en*-tohss
500	quinientos	keen-*yen*-tohss
700	setecientos	set-eh-see-*en*-tohss
900	novecientos	no-veh-see-*en*-tohss
1,000	mil	meel
2,000	dos mil	dose meel
1,000,000	un millón	oon meel-*yohn*

Colors

black	negro	*neh*-grow
blue	azul	ah-*sool*
brown	café	kah-*feh*
green	verde	*vair*-day
pink	rosa	*ro*-sah
purple	morado	mo-*rah*-doe
orange	naranja	na-*rahn*-hah
red	rojo	*roe*-hoe
white	blanco	*blahn*-koh
yellow	amarillo	ah-mah-*ree*-yoh

Days of the Week

Sunday	domingo	doe-*meen*-goh
Monday	lunes	*loo*-ness
Tuesday	martes	*mahr*-tess
Wednesday	miércoles	me-*air*-koh-less
Thursday	jueves	who-*ev*-ess
Friday	viernes	vee-*air*-ness
Saturday	sábado	*sah*-bah-doe

Months

January	enero	eh-*neh*-ro
February	febrero	feh-*brair*-oh
March	marzo	*mahr*-so
April	abril	ah-*breel*
May	mayo	*my*-oh
June	junio	*hoo*-nee-oh
July	julio	*who*-lee-yoh
August	agosto	ah-*ghost*-toe
September	septiembre	sep-tee-*em*-breh
October	octubre	oak-*too*-breh
November	noviembre	no-vee-*em*-breh
December	diciembre	dee-see-*em*-breh

Useful Phrases

Do you speak English?	¿Habla usted inglés?	*ah*-blah oos-*ted* in-*glehs*
I don't speak Spanish	No hablo español	no *ah*-blow es-pahn-*yol*
I don't understand (you)	No entiendo	no en-tee-*en*-doe
I understand (you)	Entiendo	en-tee-*en*-doe
I don't know	No sé	no *say*
I am American/ British	Soy americano(a)/ inglés(a)	soy ah-meh-ree-*kah*-no(ah)/ in-*glace*(ah)
What's your name?	¿Cómo se llama usted?	*koh*-mo say yah-mah oos-*ted*
My name is . . .	Me llamo . . .	may *yah*-moh
What time is it?	¿Qué hora es?	keh *o*-rah es
It is one, two, three . . . o'clock.	Es la una; son las dos, tres	es la *oo*-nah/*sone* lahs dose, trace
Yes, please/No, thank you	Sí, por favor/No, gracias	*see* pore fah-*vor*/no *grah*-see-us
How?	¿Cómo?	*koh*-mo
When?	¿Cuándo?	*kwahn*-doe

This/Next week	Esta semana/ la semana que entra	*es*-tah seh-*mah*-nah/lah say-*mah*-nah keh *en*-trah
This/Next month	Este mes/el próximo mes	*es*-tay mehs/el *proke*-see-mo mehs
This/Next year	Este año/el año que viene	*es*-tay *ahn*-yo/el *ahn*-yo keh vee-*yen*-ay
Yesterday/today/ tomorrow	Ayer/hoy/mañana	ah-*yair*/oy/mahn-*yah*-nah
This morning/ afternoon	Esta mañana/tarde	*es*-tah mahn-*yah*-nah/*tar*-day
Tonight	Esta noche	*es*-tah *no*-cheh
What?	¿Qué?	keh
What is it?	¿Qué es esto?	keh es *es*-toe
Why?	¿Por qué?	pore *keh*
Who?	¿Quién?	kee-*yen*
Where is . . . ?	¿Dónde está . . . ?	*dohn*-day es-*tah*
the train station?	la estación del tren?	la es-tah-see-*on* del *train*
the subway station?	la estación del Metro?	la es-ta-see-*on* del *meh*-tro
the bus stop?	la parada del autobús?	la pah-*rah*-dah del oh-toe-*boos*
the post office?	la oficina de correos?	la oh-fee-*see*-nah day koh-*reh*-os
the bank?	el banco?	el *bahn*-koh
the . . . hotel?	el hotel . . . ?	el oh-*tel*
the store?	la tienda . . . ?	la tee-*en*-dah
the cashier?	la caja?	la *kah*-hah
the . . . museum?	el museo . . . ?	el moo-*seh*-oh
the hospital?	el hospital?	el ohss-pea-*tal*
the elevator?	el ascensor?	el ah-*sen*-sore
the bathroom?	el baño?	el *bahn*-yoh
Here/there	Aquí/allá	ah-*key*/ah-*yah*
Open/closed	Abierto/cerrado	ah-be-*er*-toe/ ser-*ah*-doe

Left/right	Izquierda/derecha	iss-key-*er*-dah/ dare-*eh*-chah
Straight ahead	Derecho	der-*eh*-choh
Is it near/far?	¿Está cerca/lejos?	es-*tah* sair-kah/ *leh*-hoss
I'd like . . .	Quisiera . . .	kee-see-air-ah
a room	un cuarto/una habitación	oon *kwahr*-toe/ oo-nah ah-bee-tah-see-*on*
the key	la llave	lah *yah*-vay
a newspaper	un periódico	oon pear-ee-*oh*-dee-koh
a stamp	un timbre de correo	oon *team*-bray day koh-*reh*-oh
I'd like to buy . . .	Quisiera comprar . . .	kee-see-*air*-ah kohm-*prahr*
cigarettes	cigarrillo	ce-gar-*reel*-oh
matches	cerillos	ser-*ee*-ohs
a dictionary	un diccionario	oon deek-see-oh-*nah*-ree-oh
soap	jabón	hah-*bone*
a map	un mapa	oon *mah*-pah
a magazine	una revista	*oon*-ah reh-*veess*-tah
paper	papel	pah-*pel*
envelopes	sobres	*so*-brace
a postcard	una tarjeta postal post-*ahl*	*oon*-ah tar-*het*-ah
How much is it?	¿Cuánto cuesta?	*kwahn*-toe *kwes*-tah
It's expensive/ cheap	Está caro/barato	es-*tah* kah-roh/ bah-*rah*-toe
A little/a lot	Un poquito/ mucho . . .	oon poh-*kee*-toe/ *moo*-choh
More/less	Más/menos	mahss/*men*-ohss
Enough/too	Suficiente/de-	soo-fee-see-*en*-tay/
much/too little	masiado/muy poco	day-mah-see-*ah*-doe/*moo*-ee poh-koh
Telephone	Teléfono	tel-*ef*-oh-no
Telegram	Telegrama	teh-leh-*grah*-mah

I am ill/sick	Estoy enfermo(a)	es-*toy* en-*fair*-moh(ah)
Please call a doctor	Por favor llame un médico	pore fa-*vor* ya-may oon *med*-ee-koh
Help!	¡Auxilio! ¡Ayuda!	owk-*see*-lee-oh/ ah-*yoo*-dah
Fire!	¡Encendio!	en-*sen*-dee-oo
Caution!/Look out!	¡Cuidado!	kwee-*dah*-doh

ON THE ROAD

Highway	Carretera	car-*ray*-*ter*-ah
Causeway, paved highway	Calzada	cal-*za*-dah
Route	Ruta	*roo*-tah
Road	Camino	cah-*mee*-no
Street	Calle	*cah*-yeh
Avenue	Avenida	ah-ven-*ee*-dah
Broad, tree-lined boulevard	Paseo	pah-*seh*-oh
Waterfront promenade	Malecón	mal-lay-*cone*
Wharf	Embarcadero	em-bar-cah-*day*-ro

IN TOWN

Church	Templo/Iglesia	*tem*-plo/e-*gles*-se-*ah*
Cathedral	Catedral	cah-tay-*dral*
Neighborhood	Barrio	*bar*-re-o
Foreign exchange shop	Casa de cambio	*cas*-sah day *cam*-be-o
City hall	Ayuntamiento	ah-yoon-tah-mee-*en*-toe
Main square	Zócalo	*zo*-cal-o
Traffic circle	Glorieta	glor-e-*ay*-tah
Market	Mercado (Spanish)/	mer-*cah*-doe/
Inn	Posada	pos-*sah*-dah
Group taxi	Colectivo	co-lec-*tee*-vo

| Group taxi along fixed route | Pesero | pi-*seh*-ro |

ITEMS OF CLOTHING

Embroidered white smock	Huipil	whee-*peel*
Pleated man's shirt worn outside the pants	Guayabera	gwah-ya-*beh*-ra
Leather sandals	Huaraches	wah-*ra*-chays
Shawl	Rebozo	ray-*bozh*-o
Pancho or blanket	Serape	seh-*ra*-peh

DINING OUT

A bottle of . . .	Una botella de . . .	*oo*-nah bo-*tay*-yah deh
A cup of . . .	Una taza de . . .	*oo*-nah *tah*-sah deh
A glass of . . .	Un vaso de . . .	oon *vah*-so deh
Ashtray	Un cenicero	oon sen-ee-*seh*-roh
Bill/check	La cuenta	lah *kwen*-tah
Bread	El pan	el pahn
Breakfast	El desayuno	el day-sigh-*oon*-oh
Butter	La mantequilla	lah mahn-tay-*key*-yah
Cheers!	¡Salud!	sah-*lood*
Cocktail	Un aperitivo	oon ah-pair-ee-*tee*-voh
Dinner	La cena	lah *seh*-nah
Dish	Un plato	oon *plah*-toe
Dish of the day	El platillo de hoy	el plah-*tee*-yo day oy
Enjoy!	¡Buen provecho!	bwen pro-*veh*-cho
Fixed-price menu	La comida corrida	lah koh-*me*-dah co-*ree*-dah
Fork	El tenedor	el ten-eh-*door*
Is the tip included?	¿Está incluida la propina?	es-*tah* in-clue-*ee*-dah lah pro-*pea*-nah
Knife	El cuchillo	el koo-*chee*-yo
Lunch	La comida	lah koh-*me*-dah

Menu	La carta	lah *cart*-ah
Napkin	La servilleta	lah sair-vee-*yet*-uh
Pepper	La pimienta	lah pea-me-*en*-tah
Please give me	Por favor déme	pore fah-*vor* *day*-may
Salt	La sal	lah sahl
Spoon	Una cuchara	*oo*-nah koo-*chah*-rah
Sugar	El azúcar	el ah-*sue*-car
Waiter!/Waitress!	¡Por favor Señor/Señorita!	pore fah-*vor* sen-*yor*/sen-yor-*ee*-tah

INDEX

¿ Hablas ingués?/

¿ Habla usted inglés?

No hablo español

No entierdio (I doit understand)

Lo siento (I'm sorry)

Con permiso "pair-me-so"
                        (excuse me)

~~¿ Como está usted?~~ ¿ Como estas?

Soy Ingués(a) (I'm English)

¿ Como se llma ~~usted~~?
(what's your name?)

el baño (bathroom) por favor

Esta caro / barato (expensive / cheap)

Una botella de... agua (water)
                    mineral

Un Vaso de... vino blanco (white)
              vino espumoso (fizz)

(No) me gusta
I (don't) like it

un poco (a little)
mucho (a lot)
abierto (open) "s"errado cerrado (closed)

un café negro y un café con leche

quisiera "key see-ay-rah" (I'd like)

¿ cuánto? (how much?)

FODOR'S POCKET MEXICO CITY

EDITORS: Amy Karafin, Christine Swiac

EDITORIAL CONTRIBUTORS: Patricia Alisau, Paige Bierma, Frank Shiell

EDITORIAL PRODUCTION: Kristin Milavec

MAPS: David Lindroth, *cartographer*; Rebecca Baer, Robert Blake, *map editors*

DESIGN: Fabrizio La Rocca, *creative director*; Tigist Getachew, *art director*

PRODUCTION/MANUFACTURING: Robert B. Shields

COVER PHOTO: Peter Menzel/Stock Boston/PictureQuest

COPYRIGHT

Copyright © 2001 by Fodor's Travel Publications

Fodor's is a registered trademark of Random House, Inc. All rights reserved under International and Pan-American Copyright Conventions. Published in the United States by Fodor's Travel Publications, a division of Random House, Inc., New York, and simultaneously in Canada by Random House of Canada Limited, Toronto. Distributed by Random House, Inc., New York.

No maps, illustrations, or other portions of this book may be reproduced in any form without written permission from the publisher.

Second Edition

ISBN 0–679–00657–5

ISSN 1523–097X

IMPORTANT TIP

Although all prices, opening times, and other details in this book are based on information supplied to us at press time, changes occur all the time in the travel world, and Fodor's cannot accept responsibility for facts that become outdated or for inadvertent errors or omissions. So **always confirm information when it matters,** especially if you're making a detour to visit a specific place.

SPECIAL SALES

Fodor's Travel Publications are available at special discounts for bulk purchases for sales promotions or premiums. Special editions, including personalized covers, excerpts of existing guides, and corporate imprints, can be created in large quantities for special needs. For more information, contact your local bookseller or write to Special Markets, Fodor's Travel Publications, 280 Park Avenue, New York, NY 10017. Inquiries from Canada should be directed to your local Canadian bookseller or sent to Random House of Canada, Ltd., Marketing Department, 2775 Matheson Boulevard East, Mississauga, Ontario L4W 4P7. Inquiries from the United Kingdom should be sent to Fodor's Travel Publications, 20 Vauxhall Bridge Road, London SW1V 2SA, England.

PRINTED IN THE UNITED STATES OF AMERICA

10 9 8 7 6 5 4 3 2 1